GREAT SPORTING MOMENTS

GREAT SPORTING MOMENTS

A humorous look at some
unusual sporting incidents

SPORT

Slazenger ®

This edition specially produced in 1995 for
SARA LEE | Household & Personal Care
by arrangement with HarperCollinsPublishers
77–85 Fulham Palace Road,
Hammersmith, London W6 8JB

First published in 1993 by
Collins Willow
an imprint of HarperCollins*Publishers*

© Geoff Tibballs 1993

ISBN 0 583 32139 9

Illustrations by Richard G. Jolley

Printed and bound in Great Britain

CONTENTS

Introduction	7
Golf	9
Cricket	29
Rugby Union	63
Soccer	71
Miscellaneous Mishaps	102

INTRODUCTION

I remember the moment well. It was the first time at school that we had been told to do the hop, step and jump (an event known in more enlightened circles as the triple jump). I stood on the runway, a coiled spring waiting to explode into action and a few other mixed metaphors besides. I sprinted as fast as I could, hopped like Skippy the bush kangaroo, stepped for all I was worth and jumped higher than any salmon. I came to earth with a resounding thud, my throbbing ankle telling me that I had definitely not landed in sand. As I looked around, the reason was plain to see – I was still on the runway, four or five feet from the pit. There and then I abandoned what hopes I had of becoming the next Fred Allsop. It was another sport to add to my list of 'can't do'.

My first inkling that I was not destined for great things in the world of sport came with the awful realization that mine always seemed to be the last name called out when we picked up teams before football. I was even behind the class fatty. When I did attempt to prove my critics wrong and show my mettle as a goalkeeper, I was hindered by a full-back who insisted on telling me jokes, the punch-line invariably arriving just as the ball disappeared into the back of my net.

There were, of course, occasions when I threatened to rise above the abysmal. One lunchtime on Camber Sands, I thought I had mastered the art of off-break bowling when producing a delivery that pitched and turned to take off-stump – well, the edge of the picnic box. It was only when lying on the same stretch of beach some hours later that I realized the 'turn' may have had something to do with the fact that the beach sloped down to the sea at that point.

Then there was the time when, in a moment of recklessness, the school picked me for the cross-country team, an activity considered only marginally more offensive than being chosen for the school choir. I trailed in 15th out of 16 and would probably have fared even worse had the boy I finished ahead of not been reduced to a virtual cripple after impaling his foot on a metal spike. As it was, he nearly caught me on the run-in.

I thought that perhaps like a fine wine I might improve with age but an unorthodox golf swing which sent many a drive on to my left foot made me realize that I was really just a cheap table plonk. My final humiliation came two years ago in the fathers' race at school sports day when, dazzled by the competing array of shell suits, I came in a dismal last at the running-with-the-ball-between-your-knees race. Indeed I would still be out there now had I not picked the blessed ball up and walked the last 50 yards. My protests that it was not an officially recognized Olympic sport and how would Seb Coe have been expected to run under such a ridiculous handicap, fell on deaf ears.

People who were there that fateful afternoon still point at me in the street. My daughter hasn't spoken to me since. With that, I decided to hang up my boots, rackets and clubs and concentrate on something less energetic such as Junior Scrabble. This book is dedicated to all those who have suffered similar experiences. It is living proof that we are not alone.

Geoff Tibballs
May 1993

GOLF

SMALL MERCIES

Playing in the qualifying rounds for the 1965 Open, Walter Danecki from Milwaukee proved himself to be a golfer of quite exceptional ability. Forty-three-year-old Danecki, who had described himself on the entry form as a professional, began by recording 108 over the par 70 course at Hillside, Southport. The next day at Southport and Ainsdale, he took 113. Thus for the 36 holes, he had finished 81 over par and had the missed the qualifying total by 70 strokes. If it wasn't already obvious, it soon emerged that Walter wasn't a professional golfer at all. He had lied on the form. Why? 'Because I wanted that crock of gold.' Asked how he had enjoyed links golf, Walter unashamedly replied: 'Well I guess your small British ball helped me some. If I'd had to play the big ball, I'd have been all over the place.'

THE LEGEND OF MAURICE FLITCROFT

The exploits of Walter Danecki opened up a whole new world to rabbit golfers everywhere. Being able to take part in the Open (albeit only in the qualifying rounds) was like taking your own bat and ball to play at Lord's instead of in the park. Danecki may well have acted as inspiration for the headline-making deeds of Maurice Flitcroft, a 46-year-old crane driver from Barrow-in-Furness who took the Open by storm in 1976. Scarcely able to tame a crazy golf course let alone the windswept seaside links of Formby, Flitcroft returned a score of 121 in the first qualifying round. It transpired that he had never before played a full 18 holes of golf and, because he wasn't a member of any club, had been forced to practice on the beach. The championship committee were so aggrieved that they refunded the £30 entry fees to the two unfortunates drawn to play with him. Flitcroft, who had only been playing golf in any shape or form for 18 months, came back in 60 including a traumatic 11 at the 10th. Disappointed but better for the experience, he said: 'I've made a lot of progress in the last few months and I'm sorry I did not do better. I was trying too hard at the beginning but began to put things together at the end of the round.' But that was by no means the end of Maurice Flitcroft. He re-surfaced in 1983, calling himself Swiss professional Gerald Hoppy, and returned a 63 for a qualifying round for the Open at Pleasington. But before we despair lest this great sporting failure had suddenly acquired unsuspected prowess, it should be pointed out the 63 was for nine holes. At that point, a vigilant Royal and Ancient official politely but firmly suggested that Herr Hoppy might like to retire.

HOW NOW?

Playing the 10th hole at Guernsey in 1963, golfer S.C. King was safely on the fairway but his partner R.W. Clark was lost in the rough. After helping him to look for the ball, King returned to his own...and discovered a cow eating it. Undaunted, the intrepid duo played again the following day. This time the positions were reversed on the 10th and it was King who was deep in the rough. Before joining the search and remembering the events of the previous day, Clark took precautions by placing his woollen hat over the ball, predicting confidently: 'I'll make sure the cow doesn't eat mine.' On his return, he found that the cow had eaten his hat – although it had wisely declined to devour the pom-pom.

WRONG TRAIN

A competitor heading for the 1922 Amateur Golf Championship at Prestwick boarded a train at Ayr, confident that it would be stopping at Prestwick. To his horror, the train sailed through the station and on towards Troon further along the coast. The track runs parallel to the first hole at Prestwick and the player screamed from the passing carriage that he would be back as soon as possible. On reaching Troon, he headed back post haste but it was all in vain – he had been disqualified, having missed his starting time.

TROD ON BALL

English golfer Roger Wethered was left to rue a careless lapse in the 1921 Open at St. Andrews – one which was to cost him the championship. Weighing up a shot to the 14th in the third round, Wethered was walking backwards when he accidentally trod on his ball, thus incurring a one-stroke penalty. How costly that one shot was for at the end of 72 holes he was left tied for first place with American 'Jock' Hutchison. And it was Hutchison who went on to win the play-off.

WHAT GOES UP...

There is nothing amiss with a little gentle exuberance to celebrate a moment of sporting glory. Thus it is perfectly acceptable to leap in the air after scoring a goal or to hurl the ball skywards having taken a catch at cricket but, as Bobby Cruickshank once discovered, it is unwise to attempt a similar feat with a golf club. Playing in the final round of the 1934 US Open at Merion, Cruickshank feared the worst as his second shot to the 11th flew unerringly towards a pond. As he anticipated hearing the dreaded splash to denote that his ball had indeed found a watery grave, the fates took a hand and instead the ball hit a rock on the edge of the water and bounced on to the green. In jubilation at his escape, Cruickshank threw his club into the air but made the basic mistake of then forgetting about its trajectory. As the club descended from the heavens, Cruickshank was still applauding his good fortune...until it made a crash landing on his head.

166 ON ONE HOLE

The jewel in the crown of abysmal golfers is the unnamed woman who, in the qualifying round of the Shawnee Invitational for Ladies at Shawnee-on-Delaware, Pennsylvania, took a cool 166 strokes for the 130 yard 16th hole. Her problems began when she drove her tee shot into the Binniekill River and the ball floated downstream. Not to be denied, this resourceful woman clambered into a boat with her husband at the oars and set off in pursuit of her ball. Eventually a mile and a half further down the river, her spouse keeping score, she succeeded in beaching the ball on terra firma. But there was more drama to come since the journey back to the 16th green necessitated playing through a wood. But when you've shot the Binniekill rapids in the course of a par 3, it takes more than a few trees to deter you. And so 165 shots and nearly two hours after driving off, she holed out. It is not known whether she qualified for the later stages of the tournament.

PROBABLY THE WORST MISTAKE IN THE WORLD

Competing in the Carlsberg Women's Professional Tournament at Wolverhampton back in June 1979, Suzanne Parker completed the outward nine in 45. Alas, when it came to filling in her card, she inadvertantly put that figure in the space reserved for her score on the 9th hole. Officials ruled that the score marked on the card had to stand and so her round rocketed to 121.

COOKED HIS GOOSE

Putting on the 17th at Congressional Country Club, a Dr. Sherman A. Thomas from Washington D.C. was half-way through his backswing when a Canadian goose, lurking nearby, honked loudly as if to suggest that the ball would miss to the left. Not surprisingly, the doctor did miss the putt – but not the goose. For in a fit of pique, he pursued the bird and felled it with a blow to the head (it is not recorded which club he selected for the task). Up before the local beak, he was fined $500 for killing a goose out of season, the Federal Magistrate giving short shrift to the medical man's rather limp claim that the goose had been wounded by his approach shot and that he was merely putting it out of its misery.

HARD TO PLEASE

Most golfers would be only too delighted to get a hole in one, but not 25-year-old Mark Law. For at the time Mark, who holed out at Goring and Streatley, Oxfordshire, was taking part in a long-driving competition! He sighed: 'It was just my luck to score a hole in one when I didn't want to.'

12-PUTTED

The 1968 French Open at St. Cloud was not a happy event for Britain's Brian Barnes. After three shots to the 8th, he was just three feet from the hole but, missing one putt, he then hurriedly attempted to hit a moving ball and also incurred a penalty for standing astride the line of a putt. The result was that a further 12 shots were added to his total and he took a calamitous 15 for the hole.

GEORGIA ON HIS MIND

Tom Weiskopf is unlikely ever to forget his experience on the inglorious 12th at Augusta, Georgia, home of the US Masters. Guarded to the front by a formidable stretch of water known as Rae's Creek, the 12th has been the graveyard of many a fine player and is said to be haunted by ghosts of the Indian burial ground that was disturbed when the green was under construction. Weiskopf fell victim to the Indian sign in 1980 when he hit five balls into the creek on his way to a nightmare 13. By the second round, he had got the hang of it and improved to a seven but still felt compelled to describe it as a 'hell hole'. Every month over 5,000 reservations are made to play the hole. Just one tee shot is allowed per person and they cannot take a second shot if the ball does not land on the green. Only one in 20 need their putter.

LANDED ON THE GREENS

A member of the John O'Gaunt Club at Sutton, near Biggleswade, was dismayed to produce just about the longest drive in history– one of some 42 miles. That was because he drifted just a little way out of bounds. To be precise, his ball landed in a passing vegetable lorry and finished up in London where it fell out of a box of cabbages being unloaded at Covent Garden. Rather than wait a few days for its possible return, it is believed he played a second ball.

HARDLY WORTH TURNING UP

*P*oor *Mollie McBride might have been better off staying in bed than bothering to compete in the 1921 Canadian Ladies' Championship at Rivermead, Ottawa. For her opponent, Miss Cecil Leitch, was definitely not in a charitable frame of mind. Consequently, Mollie found herself 14 holes down at the end of the first round and after just three holes of the second round, she had succumbed to a crushing defeat by 17 and 15. Throughout the ordeal, she had held her own on just three occasions, halving two holes and actually winning the 9th. That at least was something for her to cherish.*

NO JOKE

Comedian Tim Brooke-Taylor once took 12 shots to extricate himself from a bunker on the 17th at Effingham, Surrey, while partnering Tommy Horton in the Harry Secombe Golf Classic. Tim recalls: 'I know it was 12 because a spectator reminded me 15 years later. He claims the famous Hamlet cigar commercial was based on my performance because, so he says, a representative of the advertising agency was there.'

DOUG'S DISASTER

Few who witnessed it will ever forget the torment of America's Doug Sanders in the 1970 Open at St. Andrews. He had a putt of just three feet to win the Open which was even less than Bernard Langer's infamous Ryder Cup miss in 1991. Sanders set himself up for the putt but then bent forward to remove a wisp of grass. His nerve had clearly gone and the ball duly slipped by to the right. What's more, he went on to lose the play-off to Jack Nicklaus.

HAPLESS HARRY

American professional Harry Gonder was hell bent on achieving a hole in one. So one day in 1940, armed with two witnesses and a supply of caddies to tee up and retrieve balls, he embarked on an endurance test to see how long it would take him to achieve the magic ace on a 160-yard hole. For a golfer of his standing, he thought it would be a matter of half an hour or so, certainly no more than a couple of hours. Ball after ball he hit towards the flag. His 86th attempt finished just 15 inches short but other than that, he was having difficulty finding his range. As the hours ticked by, Harry started to feel hungry and after 941 balls, he stopped for refreshment in the hope that it would change his fortunes. It so nearly worked for his 996th hit the pin and bounced three inches away. On and on he went. At 8.10pm, his 1,162nd shot stopped six inches short and, beginning to get into his stride at last, his 1,184th missed by three inches. It was a false dawn. As the church bells struck midnight, Harry struck his 1,600th ball. Like most of its predecessors, it finished nowhere near the target. By now fatigue was beginning to set in and a nasty blister appeared on his hand. Still he battled on and was so nearly rewarded twice in the space of a few minutes. His 1,750th hit the pin as did the 1,756th which ended up just one measly inch from the hole. That seemed to convince Harry that even if he carried on into 1941, he was never going to get that elusive hole in one. At 2.40am, 16 hrs 25mins after he had first teed off, Harry's 1,817th shot finished ten long feet from the pin...and he gave up.

LEAST HOSPITABLE COURSE

A course to avoid at all costs is the one which opened in Kenya in the 1960s. One of the rules states that if your ball lands on or by a crocodile, you have the option of moving the ball a club's length away – or moving the crocodile.

THE MAN FROM DEL MONTE

Curiously in golf it is often a case of the shorter the hole, the bigger the headache. Take American Hans Merell who, on 17 January 1959 during the third round of the BingCrosby National Tournament at Del Monte, California, managed to take 19 to complete the 222-yard par-3 16th.

BIG BUILD-UP

The Australian PGA event was once started by a colourful
individual who insisted on giving the golfers a Palladium-
style introduction as they stood on the first tee. 'Next from
Nationalist China,' he proclaimed, 'we have Cho Ling-Low.
He doesn't swing the scales far, but my word, would you
watch him hit this one.' Poor Mr. Cho, barely 5ft tall, was
sadly unable to live up to his newly-acquired reputation as
one of the game's big hitters. His drive bounced three times
before trickling into the 200-yard cross bunkers.

ROUGH JUSTICE

The least successful ruling in the history of golf must be
that which a US Open official tried to impose on
Walter Hagen in the 1919 tournament. On the 17th hole
of the play-off, Hagen had sliced into the rough and his
ball ended up on a patch of extremely soft ground. It was
found embedded in the mud amidst claims that it had
been trodden on by members of the gallery. Nevertheless
the official ruled that the ball should be played as it was.
Hagen protested and asked to identify the ball. The
official agreed and turned the ball over a number of times
but still Hagen maintained that he was not convinced
that it was his. By the time Hagen accepted the
situation, most of the mud had been removed by the
somewhat gullible official. The soil around was loose
and the ball was once more playable .

UNLUCKY JIM

Surrey pub landlord Jim Meade expected stiff competition on
his golfing society's day out. What he didn't expect was to
land up in hospital after being knocked out twice in a matter

of seconds by flying golf balls. Jim was minding his own business searching for his ball in the rough when from an adjoining fairway a ball hurtled through the trees, ricocheted off a branch and hit him between the eyes. As people rushed to Jim's aid and helped him to his feet, he was immediately struck again by another player's sliced drive. He ended up needing four stitches to his forehead and was left with a bump which appropriately was the size of a golf ball. Battered and bruised, Jim said: 'I can't believe this has happened to me. I thought I was in a war zone. I didn't know much about the first strike, but two of the lads were helping me to my feet when there was another shout of fore. They hit the deck, left me staggering about and the ball whacked me in the middle of the back. I stumbled, went down again and just flaked out. Now they want me to hold the flag on every hole so they can be sure of hitting the target!'

DOWN TO EARTH

The experiences of Tommy Armour in 1927 amply illustrate the ups and downs of golf. Just a week after winning the US Open, Armour was playing in the Shawnee Open. But any hopes he had of repeating his triumph were shattered at the 17th at which he took 23 strokes, hooking a succession of balls out of bounds.

SEX CHANGE

About to tee off at the start of the Glen Campbell Los Angeles open, Clive Clark stepped forward to hear the starter proclaim: 'And next on the tee from London, England, we have Olive Clark.'

ONE MAN WENT TO MOW

Many people remarked about the length of the grass on the Lindrick greens for the first day of the 1957 Ryder Cup. The reason was simple – the greenkeeper at the Yorkshire club thought the competition was starting a day later than it was. In the circumstances, I suppose the United States and Great Britain teams were lucky they didn't have to wave through a ladies' foursomes.

COOK ROASTED

Eight holes up with just eight to play at the Army Golf Club, Aldershot, on 5 July 1974, Mike Cook already had one hand on the coveted Gradoville Bowl. Then in the manner of all great sporting failures, he fell apart completely, allowing his opponent, M.C. Smart, to win every remaining hole. By now thoroughly dejected, Cook also threw in the first play-off hole for good measure.

HOLE IN ONE

Driving off the first tee at Blackmoor Golf Club at Bordon, Hampshire, a player was amazed to see his ball disappear down the hole. Unfortunately, it was the hole of a chimney 120 yards away and 40 yards out of bounds on the right. It also came as quite a surprise to the owner of the house and his wife who were sitting in front of the fire at the time.

SECOND-CLASS MALE

In the 1950s, one Colonel H. Nugent-Head, a noted long hitter and it would seem something of a chauvinist, proudly boasted that no woman could beat him on any course playing level. He found a filly that was prepared to take him on, a lady by the name of Frances Stephens, and no doubt to a crescendo of cheers from lady golfers, she beat him 3 and 2.

SUPERGRASS

British golfer Jamie Spence left the third round of the 1993 Rome Masters as joint-leader and on the way to the chance of a £50,000 payout. But his hopes were dashed by an eagle-eyed spectator who had seen Spence mistakenly drop in the wrong place off a path and had felt it his duty to tell an official. Four hours after his round had been completed, the luckless Spence was hauled back to the course to undergo trial by television. Having watched the action replay, the organizers disqualified him for signing for a score which did not include a two-stroke penalty.

JUST TOO LATE

Brigadier-General Critchley had set his heart on competing in the 1937 Amateur Championship at Sandwich. And to prove it he was travelling all the way from New York to take part. Unfortunately, his Atlantic crossing on the Queen Mary was delayed by fog and the ship was therefore late docking at Southampton. However the military man was nothing if not well-prepared and had taken the precaution of hiring an aeroplane to take him to Sandwich. Realizing he was cutting it fine as he reached the Kent coast, he circled over the clubhouse so that officials knew his arrival would be imminent. But in golf, rules are rules and there is no room for sentiment. The Brigadier-General did make it to the clubhouse but he was a whole six minutes late and his name had been irrevocably struck out. At the same championship, an entrant from Burma who had travelled across the Pacific and the American continent, also had the misfortune to be on board the fog-bound Queen Mary. He lacked the far-sightedness of Brigadier-General Critchley and travelled from Southampton to Sandwich by car, eventually arriving four hours after his allocated starting time. Despite having trekked half-way around the world, he too was struck out. It must have been a long journey home.

POLITICAL APOLOGY

Former US Vice President Spiro Agnew was at his most dangerous with a golf club in his hand. His hook was deadlier than Henry Cooper's. It was because organizers knew that there would never be a dull moment, nor a spectator standing, when Agnew was around that he became much in demand for celebrity tournaments. Agnew didn't mind who he hit – professional golfers and ordinary members of the public came alike to him. Once at the Bob Hope Classic, one of his trademark wayward shots struck Doug Sanders on the head. Rushing out a letter of apology (it was rumoured he had them ready-printed), he also sent Sanders a memento of the occasion in the form of a silver tray on which was engraved in large letters the word 'FORE'.

JACK'S OFF DAY

Just to prove that even the mighty are human, Jack Nicklaus shot an inspired 83 in the first round of the 1981 Open at Royal St. George's, Sandwich. And he only achieved that by completing the last four holes in level par. He had four double-bogeys and his piece de resistance, giving hope to millions, was a tee shot on the par-5 14th which travelled no further than 80 yards. After what was at the time his worst-ever round as a professional golfer, the usually co-operative Nicklaus declined to give any press interviews for fear that he might say something he would later regret. His score sent shock waves around the world of golf and on the television news that night, it was mentioned even before that of the leader.

FALSE ALARM

The Point Grey Golf and Country Club in Vancouver, British Columbia, reacted swiftly to news that a golfer had suffered a heart attack out on the course. They immediately notified the emergency services and sure enough within minutes an ambulance crew was on the scene to tend to the patient. But as it turned out, they need not have hurried. The alarm had been raised after a passing golfer had noticed 95-year-old Justice J.M. Coody, a retired member of British Columbia's Supreme Court, resting in a golf buggy. The man asked what the problem was and he thought the judge replied, 'Heart failure'. He hadn't. In fact,

*the only likely demise was that of Justice Coody's buggy
which had stalled. And what he had actually said was,
'Cart failure'.*

BUNKERED!

Amateur golfer Melville Bucher was thoroughly
enjoying playing with the big boys in the 1955 Open
at St. Andrews. He had survived the cut and made it
through to the final round where, whilst not exactly
threatening the leader board, he was going along
merrily enough. Until the par-3 11th that is. For there
he put his tee shot into the awkward Strath bunker. At
one point Mr. Bucher must have thought he was going
to be like Hitler and never get out of the bunker but
finally six shots later he emerged. However, he finished
up taking ten for the hole and ruined an otherwise
respectable round.

OH DEER

A natural hazard of playing Wollaton Park Golf Club in
Nottingham is the herd of red deer that wanders the
course. Most of the year they sit quietly in the rough or
under trees but come the rutting season they are a different
proposition altogether. So when two golfers strolled around
the course blissfully unaware of the deer calendar, they
thought nothing of the fact that their shots had landed right
next to a huge stag. And they didn't think much of it when
the stag, which seemed to be carrying a full set of clubs on
its head, menacingly chased them towards the green. Wisely
they decided to abandon a lost cause and agreed on a free
drop the other side of the fairway.

MID-AIR COLLISION

During the 1980 Corfu International Championship, Sharon Peachey saw her drive collide in mid-air with a ball from a competitor playing a different hole. Not only did Sharon lose vital yardage but her ball finished up in a pond!

DEVLIN'S DIP

Coming to the 18th in the 1975 San Diego Open at Torrey Pines, Australia's Bruce Devlin was right up there in the prize money. But that hole was to prove a blow to his pride and to his wallet. For, having landed in a shallow pond, Devlin made the mistake of thinking that he could somehow play his way out. He waded in and, wielding his club, started to splash around frantically without ever making much contact with the ball. When all hope seemed lost, he did eventually emerge – but it was six shots later. And the 10 he took for the 18th cost him $3,000. Course officials were so taken by Devlin's single-minded determination flying in the face of common sense that they decided to erect a plaque at the scene of the mayhem, christening it 'Devlin's Pond'. To his credit, Devlin himself saw the amusing side but suggested Australianizing it to 'Devlin's Billabong'.

BLIND DATE

Former US Open Champion J.J. McDermott must have forgotten to look at his diary before travelling to Britain to compete in the qualifying rounds for the 1914 Open at Prestwick. For he got the wrong week and having journeyed across the Atlantic, he arrived on the very day that qualifying finished.

CRUEL LUCK

Competing in the prestigious Tournament Players Championship at Sydney in 1989, Australia's Bob Emond enjoyed the sort of excursions on a par-5 normally reserved for the humblest Sunday morning golfer. Once he had landed in the water for the fourth time, he knew it was going to be one of those holes. Thoroughly miserable, he made matters worse by allowing one of his penalty drops to hit his shoe, thereby incurring a further two-stroke loss. By now he had taken 11 and was still nowhere near the green. Manfully he struggled on, only to suffer a further self-inflicted wound when collecting another two-stroke penalty (his 15th and 16th shots) for marking a ball that was not on the green. Finally, he three putted for a 19. His reaction was unprintable.

A FAIR COP

Just about the unluckiest burglars in the annals of crime were the pair who in 1989 decided to rob a house bordering Warley Park Golf Club in Essex. They were caught in the act by no fewer than 24 off-duty policemen out on a golf day!

SOAKED TO THE SKIN

Surely the least successful autograph hunters in the world were those who surrounded Gary Player in 1976 as he came off the 18th green at the Congressional Country Club following a practice round. Such was the clamour for the South African's signature that in the ensuing scrimmage the boys accidentally pushed him in a lake!

IT'S A KNOCKOUT

Selecting a wood to drive off the 17th tee at Lyme Regis, Dorset, 69-year-old Derek Gatley was half-way through his backswing when the steel shaft snapped and the club struck him on the back of the head, knocking him out. When he came to, Mr Gatley admitted: 'It was the first thing I had hit all day!'

PROFESSIONAL HIT-MAN

As he stood on the 18th tee at St. Margaret's-at-Cliffe in Kent, club professional W.J. Robinson was supremely confident of clearing the cow which was grazing 100 yards up the fairway. But this bovine hazard proved more than a match for Robinson whose drive clattered into the unsuspecting creature. Sadly the cow was killed, leaving Robinson with what can only be described as an awkward second shot.

HERMAN MONSTER

Troon's famous 126-yard 8th, otherwise known as the Postage Stamp because of its miniscule green, has destroyed many a reputation. And it didn't do much for the prospects of German amateur Herman Tissies who, competing in the first qualifying round for the 1950 Open, took a monstrous 15. Having missed the green with his tee-shot, Herr Tissies proceeded to spend several minutes zig-zagging across the sward from bunker to bunker, presumably in search of one he liked. Finally, he managed to stop his 14th stroke on the green. Just when it seemed that spectators would be in for another treat watching the German attempt to hole out, he spoiled their fun by one-putting.

CRICKET

EXPENSIVE DELIVERY

The stage was set for an enthralling encounter between Western Australians, Bunbury and a visiting touring team from Victoria. Bunbury's opening bowler steamed in to deliver the first ball of the match...which was promptly despatched into a three-pronged branch of a tall Jarrah tree. And there it sat. The home side desperately claimed that it was a lost ball, but the umpire decreed that it was not lost because it could be seen, those being the quaint rules in days of old. Meanwhile, the Victoria batsmen continued to run. By now the Bunbury players were beside themselves. They tried to resort to drastic measures by sending for an axe to fell the tree but none could be found. Finally, someone produced a rifle and the ball was shot down from its perch. Alas, by the time it had been returned to the middle, the batsmen had run 286. It will come as no surprise to learn that Victoria went on to win comfortably.

ILLUSTRIOUS CAREER

When the names of great Australian cricketers are under discussion, for some reason it is always the likes of Bradman, Benaud and Lillee that spring to the fore. Only rarely does that of Dr. R.L. Park warrant a mention. Perhaps this is because in his solitary Test appearance against England at Melbourne in 1920, the hapless medic was out first ball in his only innings and delivered a solitary over which cost his side nine runs. He was said to be disappointed at not being selected again.

LAMBS TO THE SLAUGHTER

*F*acing a target of 133, Seaham Harbour were skittled for just one run by Gateshead Fell in the Durham Under-18 League...and even that came from a leg bye. It was a case of trial by ordeal as Seaham, some of whose batsmen were only 11, wilted in the face of a furious onslaught launched by 16-year-olds Neil Killeen and Steve Lugsden, both Durham county players who have appeared in Gateshead Fell's first team. Nine of the youngsters were clean bowled and the tenth was run out, making a rare sortie from the crease, as the Seaham innings lasted a mere nine overs. It was thought that he had simply been trying to escape to the safety of the pavilion. Shortly before proceedings came to a merciful climax, two brave souls had successfully ventured down the wicket to scamper a leg bye, much to the disgust of Gateshead's demonic duo. Steve Lugsden moaned: 'I was upset when they got their run – I wanted to get them out for nothing.' Seaham secretary Jim Dyson said of the debacle in May 1993: 'It was sheer terror for most of our lads. Some were so scared they almost stood beside the square leg umpire as the bowlers ran in!'

BROKE HIS DUCK

In 1990, Northamptonshire tail-ender Mark Robinson had enjoyed a less than glorious summer with the bat. From 4 May he went 12 first-class innings without scoring a run until finally on 15 September, he rounded off the season with a magnificent 1 not out which played no small part in helping his side to victory over Leicestershire. Suggestions that the run was a gift were hastily dismissed and Robinson, cheered all the way back to the pavilion, declared: 'It was one of the proudest moments of my life.'

GREEN'S HOUSE EFFECT

When Walsden entertained Rochdale in a Central Lancashire League match, Walsden bowler Peter Green was hit for a massive six by Rochdale batsman Wilson Hartley. The ball sailed out of the ground and smashed through the window of a house in an adjoining street. To add insult to injury, it was Peter Green's house.

SHORTEST MATCH

A supposed friendly between a team of Fijians and Europeans, the latter under the captaincy of the Hon. J.A. Udal, on the island of Taveuni in 1906 was abandoned after just one ball had been bowled. It had dismissed the local High Chief who was so irate at being out that it was deemed prudent not to proceed further with the game.

WORST TEST FIGURES

The distinction of achieving the worst bowling figures in Test match history goes to the hitherto unsung L.O.B. 'Chuck' Fleetwood-Smith, an Australian left-arm spinner. Playing against England at the Oval in 1938, his sustained spell didn't exactly succeed in tying the home bats men down. England declared at 903–7 and Fleetwood-Smith finished with the highly forgettable figures of 1–298.

TOO SMALL FOR HIS BOOTS

Even the greatest of players have their off days. Take Denis Compton about to make his MCC debut against Suffolk at Felixstowe. Later renowned for being not exactly the most organized of individuals, young Compton arrived at the ground to discover that he had left his cricket bag at Lord's. Consequently, he was obliged to take the field in kit borrowed from a player seven inches taller than himself and who took two-and-a-half-boot sizes larger. The suspicion that Compton would have been more comfortable in a suit of armour was reinforced when, scarcely able to move about the crease, he was not altogether surprisingly bowled first ball.

OUT OF POCKET

Village teams can always rely on special fund-raising matches to acquire essential extra revenue for ground maintenance. Thus in 1989, Twyford CC near Bristol staged

*just such a fixture which brought in a much-needed £44.
Unfortunately in the course of the match a window was
broken by a six and the club had to fork out £45 to repair it!*

SWIFT DEPARTURE

Informed sources tell of the occasion when Henry Tubb
of Free Foresters and Oxford University swung a
mighty blow which looked to be going clean out of the
ground until it struck a swift in flight and rebounded
into the hands of a surprised fielder.

TURNING A DEAF EAR

The First Test between England and Australia at Trent
Bridge in 1953 saw Australia floundering at 81–6 in their
second innings. The evening gloom was gathering over
Nottingham and so as Don Tallon, Australia's wicket-keeper
who was known to be hard of hearing, left the pavilion to bat,
his captain Lindsay Hassett shouted after him: 'Deafy, give

the light a go,' meaning that Tallon should appeal against the light. However Tallon mis-heard the instructions as 'have a go' and proceeded to launch into an inexplicable and frenzied attack upon the English bowling before holing out for a quick-fire 15 while attempting another big hit. Australia were duly bowled out for 123 but, despite Tallon's efforts, managed to hold on for a draw.

TOO DRUNK TO BOWL

Yorkshire and England left-arm spinner Bobby Peel was booted out of the game in the 1890s by his county captain Lord Hawke after Peel had walked on to the field too drunk to know in which direction he was supposed to be bowling. Hawke, a disciplinarian who would have made Cromwell seem the life and soul of the party, later explained by way of absolution: 'It had to be done for the sake of discipline and for the good of cricket.'

BURNT OUT

Batting at Kalgoorlie, Australia, in the 1970s, one Stan Dawson was struck by a speedy delivery that promptly ignited a box of matches which he had secreted in his hip pocket. To add to his woe, Dawson was run out as he tried to beat down the flames.

DISMISSED HIMSELF

Tailender James Southerton insisted he was out during a match at The Oval in 1870 and stalked off while the umpire tried to call him back. It went into the scorebook as 'J. Southerton, retired thinking he was out.'

OUT ON BAIL?

*W*hen England toured Australasia in 1877, they were
horrified to learn that the First Test in Melbourne was to
take place virtually as soon as they had disembarked after
the boat crossing from New Zealand. As it was, half of the
team took the field suffering from sea-sickness while their
only wicket-keeper, Edward Pooley, was languishing in a
Christchurch jail. Before one of the matches played in New
Zealand, he had struck up a bet with a local gambler as to
how many Christchurch batsmen would score ducks. Pooley
reckoned he was owed nearly £9 but the gambler welshed on
the deal. The resulting argument ended in fisticuffs and both
men were jailed pending a trial. By the time Pooley was
acquitted, his team-mates had lost the First Test by 45 runs.

OF LITTLE BENEFIT

A benefit match has always been the icing on the cake
for professional cricketers, a fitting reward for years
of sterling service. So naturally Somerset's Bertie Buse
was eagerly anticipating his chosen fixture, against
Lancashire in 1953, in the hope that the weather would
stay fine for the three days and thus bring out the
crowds. Before the match, actor Arnold Ridley (later of
Dad's Army fame) wrote in an open letter to Buse:
'Good luck to your benefit. May you score plenty of
runs and get busy among the wickets.' But, disastrously
for Buse's pocket, he got a little too busy among the
wickets, contributing to his own downfall by removing
six Lancashire batsmen. As a result, the game was all
over in a day with Somerset taking advantage of an
awkward pitch to triumph by an innings and 24 runs. So
whilst expressing sympathy for Buse, it has to be said
that it was something of a self-inflicted wound.

MORBID SCORECARD

Playing in the final of the 1958–59 Qaid-I-Azam Trophy in Karachi, Abdul Aziz was injured in the first innings. The scorecard thus read: 'Abdul Aziz retired hurt...0.' The injury proved to be fatal and the scorer, obviously not wishing to leave any room for doubt, wrote for the second innings: 'Abdul Aziz did not bat, dead...0'.

HASTY EXIT

England's 1959–60 tour of the West Indies was marred by disgraceful riot scenes in Port of Spain. Bottles and seats were hurled onto the pitch, observed by the keen eye of BBC radio commentator Rex Alston. 'I've never seen anything like it in my life,' he broadcast. 'The crowd away to my right are behaving like a lot of hooligans.' Unfortunately for Alston, the said crowd were tuned in to his commentary on their transistor radios and on hearing his words of condemnation, they turned towards the derelict commentary box in anger. Alston and his colleagues were forced to flee to safety as the old box was reduced to a pile of rubble in little more than 30 seconds.

ONE-BALL DEFEAT

Spectators assembled for the York Senior League fixture between Cawood and Dringhouses in August 1979 expecting a closely-fought contest. But it looked rather ominous for Dringhouses when their entire team were bowled out for just 2. Hopes of similar reprisals proved remarkably short-lived since the first delivery of Cawood's reply flew past the wicket-keeper for four byes. Thus

Cawood had won without actually hitting a ball.
A Dringhouses player conceded that 'probably the better
team won on the day.'

SOUVENIR HUNTER

When England toured Australia in 1886–87, they were supposed to be playing a Combined Australia XI at Melbourne. However, the leading lights of New South Wales were not available so instead the English and Victorian teams were divided up into Smokers and Non-Smokers and a match was arranged between them. This contrived spectacle proved of absolutely no interest whatsoever to the Melbourne public, the attendance on the final day barely reaching 100. It was so forgettable that Victoria's W.H. Scotton, who was batting at the time, decided he would like the match ball as a souvenir of the occasion. At the end of play he picked it up, only to be given out by a fussy umpire (probably one who had just given up smoking) as 'handled ball'.

IGUANA STOPPED PLAY

The First Test between Young Sri Lanka and Young England in 1987 was briefly halted when a large iguana crept sinisterly across the square at the Colombo Cricket Club ground.

NO-WIN SITUATION

Centuries are far too commonplace to be remotely interesting, but one that would have been worthy of international acclaim was that attempted by

Northamptonshire in the late 1930s. Over four painstaking years, longer even than a Trevor Bailey hundred, Northants crawled their way towards a century of successive County Championship matches without a win. Their 'innings' began following victory over Somerset at Taunton on 14 May 1935 and continued effortlessly through their next 99 Championship fixtures (61 of them defeats). Then, agonisingly one short of their ton, they ended up beating Leicestershire by an innings in two days at Northampton on 29 May 1939.

UMPIRE CONFUSED

When Barbados met British Guiana in 1946, the umpires, accustomed to usually counting up to six, found great difficulty adjusting to the eight-ball over which was in force at the time. One over from Guiana's D.F. Hill, which contained neither wides nor no-balls, was allowed to continue unhindered for 14 deliveries. The umpire's miscalculation might have gone unnoticed had he had not given Everton Weekes out lbw to the 14th ball.

PRIDE BEFORE A FALL

It takes a team particularly adept in the art of failure to lose a match having bowled out the opposition for 15. But Warwickshire managed it with runs to spare in their County Championship fixture with Hampshire at Edgbaston in 1922. Having compiled a respectable 223 in their first innings, Warwickshire skittled the men from the south coast for a paltry 15. At the end of that first day, the Warwickshire captain, the Hon. F.S. Calthorpe, was naturally in bullish mood and suggested to his opposite number, the Hon. L.H. Tennyson, that when the match was over, the amateurs should play each other at golf. However, Tennyson was none too amused by the proposal and, apparently in language not appropriate to his social standing, he bet Calthorpe £10 that Hampshire would win the cricket match. Calthorpe must have thought he was on to easy money, only to see Hampshire, following-on, rattle up 521 and then bowl out Warwickshire for 158 in their second innings to gain an unlikely victory by 155 runs.

WICKETLESS

At Old Trafford in 1956, Leicestershire contrived to lose to Lancashire without taking a wicket in the entire match. Lancashire declared their first innings at 166–0 and knocked off the 66 required to wrap up a ten-wicket victory, again without being troubled by the feeble visiting attack.

BAD HAND SIGNALS

With his team batting, Ray East, the Essex Second XI coach, was sitting in the dressing-room when the phone rang. The call was for one of the Essex players, who could be *seen in the distance meandering aimlessly around the boundary. Taking a leaf out of Lionel Blair's book, East mimed through the dressing-room door to get the player to the phone and then sat back in his chair again. Barely a minute had elapsed when instead of the wanted man, the two batsmen walked into the dressing-room. 'Lunch already, lads?' inquired East. 'No,' replied one, 'we've declared, haven't we? Wasn't that you waving us in?'*

'QUICKEST' PAIR

Glamorgan's Peter Judge had an unfortunate experience at the hands of Indian bowler Sarwate when the tourists visited Cardiff. Last man in for the county, Judge was bowled first ball by Sarwate and, to save time when Glamorgan followed-on, he kept his pads on and stayed at the crease to open the second innings. Again, Judge was clean bowled by Sarwate first ball.

MISTAKEN IDENTITY

In 1899, Narraway's Farm at Acton was scheduled to be the venue for two matches. Kildare II were due to entertain Crescent of Hampstead while on an adjoining pitch, Kildare III were to meet Crofton from Streatham. But when the two visiting teams arrived, they each mistook the other for Kildare . The captains of Crescent and Crofton managed to exchange introductions without identifying themselves, tossed for first innings and the batsmen marched out to the middle. The first ball was about to be bowled when a Kildare player turned up and wondered why he didn't recognize any of his team-mates. When he passed on his concern to the umpires, proceedings were halted in the nick of time.

OFF THE OVER

*B*owling in a Queensland country match during season
1968–69, R. Grubb achieved the memorable feat of
conceding 62 runs in one eight-ball over. Batsman H. Morley
struck nine sixes and two fours off the over which included
four no-balls.

CURIOUS DISMISSAL

*S*urrey opening batsman Laurie Fishlock was eager to
capitalize on a no-ball which came his way during
the match with Kent at the Oval in 1938. He advanced
boldly down the wicket and launched himself into a
full-blooded drive. Perhaps he overdid the aggression
for as he swung at the ball, his bat snapped in two.
Consequently, he got only the faintest of touches which
carried through to the quick-thinking wicket-keeper
who caught the ball and broke the wicket. A batsman
cannot be out caught or stumped from a no-ball but
Fishlock, with no bat to ground, had to return to the
pavilion, adjudged run out.

GO SLOW

*T*he noble game of cricket isn't just about frantic limited-
over run chases – the science of stone-walling also has a
valuable if unproductive part to play. The dead bat was
witnessed at its finest during a Yorkshire League match
between Green Hammerton, near York, and Headingley
Broomfield in 1976. Set 181 to win, Green Hammerton had
slumped to an alarming 14–8. It was fair to say that victory
seemed unlikely so batsmen Tom Bell and Ken Kershaw
decided to close ranks and bat out the remaining 75 minutes

in the hope of securing a draw. Bell said later: 'We just put our heads down and we stopped.' While the spectators somehow managed to contain their excitement, the dour duo stayed through 33 successive maiden overs until Kershaw was finally prised out. In marched the last man, Mark Williams, but Bell, fearful that the newcomer might not even be able to block adequately, made the fatal mistake of trying to score a run in order to keep the strike. Attempting to scoop a single back over the bowler's head, Bell was caught and bowled by a Mr. Z. Ali who finished with the economical figures of 14–14–0–1. Green Hammerton had succumbed with just two minutes' playing time left. When the scorebook was examined, it revealed that there were 288 balls in the Green Hammerton innings – and runs were scored from just eight.

TATE'S TORMENT

Few Test careers have been as miserable as that of 35-year-old Sussex bowler Fred Tate. Called up as a last-minute replacement against Australia at Old Trafford in 1902, he dropped a crucial catch, hardly bowled despite the wet conditions and had to go in last when England needed just eight runs to win. He made four but was then bowled, giving Australia victory by three runs. Poor Fred was never forgiven and it remained his one and only Test.

WASHOUT

Plans to stage an indoor cricket match at Basingstoke in 1993 were scuppered when the game was rained off. The pitch was flooded after water had poured through a hole in the sports hall roof.

LEAST SPORTING GESTURE

*P*assions ran high during the 1991 final of India's Duleep Trophy when West Zone bowler Rashid Patel aimed a head-high full toss at North Zone batsman Raman Lamba. The latter showed his displeasure, at which Patel uprooted a stump and attacked Lamba with it. Mercifully, this sort of cricketing vandalism is usually confined to a hot day on Blackpool beach.

UNSUCCESSFUL EXPERIMENT

*S*ometimes in the field of sport, it really does pay to stick to what you do best, a fact to which Glamorgan's Malcolm Nash would surely testify. A 23-year-old fast medium left-arm bowler of some promise, Nash decided to experiment with a slower style against Nottinghamshire at Swansea on 31 August 1968. Notts' West Indian Test star Garfield Sobers responded by hitting each of Nash's deliveries for six, taking a maximum 36 off the over. Nash remained philosophical, conceding: 'I suppose I can gain some consolation from the fact that my name will be permanently in the record books.'

MEMORABLE CAREER

If Gloucestershire batsman Sidney George Wells had ever recounted tales of his cricketing life in print, it would have been a slim volume indeed. For his exploits in the first-class game were a tableau of inactivity – in fact it is questionable whether he actually set foot on the pitch. Sidney's career consisted of just one appearance, against Kent at Bristol in 1927, but the match was abandoned without a ball being bowled!

MIS-MATCH OF THE DAY

Dera Ismail Khan knew they faced stiff opposition when taking on Pakistan Western Railways in an Ayub Trophy match at Lahore in December 1964 but even they couldn't have expected it to turn out quite so one-sided. Batting first, Railways piled up the runs and occupied the crease until lunch on the third day at which point they declared at 910–6. After so long in the field and faced with a veritable mountain to climb even to save the follow-on, perhaps it was inevitable that Dera Ismail Khan should wilt. And wilt they did. They were rapidly bowled out for 32 and 27 to go down by the fairly conclusive margin of an innings and 851 runs. It was Dera Ismail Khan's first and last first-class match.

THE UPS AND DOWNS OF CRICKET

Contemporary reports tell of a fine game of cricket played at Chatham Lines, Kent, back in the 1880s. One side amassed a moderately respectable 46, only for their opponents to win with a single hit. The lucky strike sent the ball rolling down to the foot of a steep hill known as the Brook. A posse of fielders set off in pursuit and positioned themselves *along the hillside, the idea being that they would throw the ball to each other in relays prior to returning it to the middle. However, the tactic ended in abysmal failure as some of the relay catchers had an unfortunate tendency to drop the ball, at which point it rolled back down to the bottom of the hill. While this lengthy retrieval process was being effected, the batsmen were trotting up and down at their leisure to compile the 47 runs necessary for victory. A similar tale comes from a match played on Beacon Hill near the Sussex village of Rottingdean where no fewer than 67 runs were scored off a single hit. The ball raced down the hill to the village where again a relay system of fielders set about organizing its rapid return. But these players had much safer hands and the conveyer belt looked to be doing a competent job until they were let down in spectacular fashion by the last man in the line. It was his task to throw the ball in to the wicket-keeper, but tragically his return was too high and the keeper could only look on in anguish as the ball sailed over his head and rolled down the other side of the hill...*

SAD DISMISSAL

Playing against Somerset at Taunton on 22 May 1919, Sussex's H.J. Heygate was given out because he failed to reach the crease within two minutes of the fall of the previous wicket. Poor Heygate was crippled with rheumatism and couldn't make it to the middle when the ninth Sussex wicket fell in their second innings. He was shown on the scorecard as 'absent'.

EIGHT MEN SHORT

Kent were all set to take the field for the second day of their County Championship match with Middlesex at Tunbridge Wells in June 1963 when they realized that only three of the Middlesex team were present. The rest had been stuck in heavy traffic. The trio were one batsman who was not out, one who had already been out and the 12th man. The not out player, Bob White, thought he might as well get padded up and wait in the middle in the hope that a partner might soon arrive. With the Kent fielders idling their time looking for someone to bowl to, the umpires decided they could wait no longer and officially closed the Middlesex innings. Kent then came out to bat ten minutes later with many of their number being temporarily loaned to Middlesex as fielders. Indeed one, Prodger, standing at second slip, had the distinction of catching his own team-mate Brian Luckhurst! The fun ended when the other Middlesex players turned up and it settled down to another routine county game.

PLUCK OF THE IRISH

*T*he proudest day in the annals of Irish cricket spectacularly coincided with just about the most humiliating one in the history of the West Indies. In 1969, fielding six of the team which had drawn the previous day's Test with England (including the likes of Clive Lloyd, Basil Butcher, Joey Carew and John Shepherd), the West Indies were skittled for 25 by Ireland in a one-day match at Londonderry. It could have been even worse for at one point the West Indies were 12–9. Ireland went on to complete a memorable nine-wicket victory. The steel bands were silent that night.

GONE TO LUNCH

When Sussex entertained Kent at Brighton in August 1891, the lunchtime fare provided at the ground apparently held little appeal for the gourmet palate of the visitors' C.J.M. Fox, so he went elsewhere for lunch. He partook of such a sumptuous repast that by the time he had returned to the action, the Kent innings had ended and he had been given out 'absent'.

THREE DUCKS IN ONE MATCH

It is no mean feat to be dismissed three times in a match without scoring but what makes this particular deed of incompetence all the more praiseworthy is that it happened to none other than Viv Richards. Even at the tender age of 18, Richards was worshipped by cricket-lovers in Antigua. And the crowd were looking forward to another peerless display from the youngster when he walked to the crease to face St. Kitts in the 1969 Leeward Islands Tournament at Antigua Recreation Ground. So imagine their disgust when he was given out fourth ball to a dubious bat-pad catch. Never ones to hide their emotions, the Antiguan spectators promptly brought the match to a halt. The umpires, appreciating the delicate nature of the situation, amazingly agreed to give Antigua's favourite son another chance. Richards duly re-emerged...but was soon out stumped. This time there was no controversy. Nor was there in the second innings when he was again out for nought to complete a treble failure.

CONSISTENTLY BAD

A cricket club from North-East Lancashire calling themselves The Untouchables established a splendid sequence of ineptitude between 1945 and 1956. In the course of those 12 seasons, they played 127 games and never once managed to register a win. They lost 109 and drew the remainder. On one occasion when they needed just nine runs to win with six wickets standing and victory at last appeared within their grasp, they sensibly collapsed in the nick of time to ensure that their record remained intact.

NEW ZEALAND'S FINEST HOUR

The gallant batsmen of New Zealand wrote their way into the record books with a stunning display of inefficiency in the Second Test against England at Eden Park, Auckland, on 28 March 1955. It had all started tediously enough. In their first innings New Zealand made an adequate 200 and England replied with 246. Little could the tourists have known that such a slender lead would be sufficient for them not to have to bat again. For when New Zealand took to the crease second time around, they were routed for an all-time Test record low of 26 in just 27 overs. Sadly, the symmetry of the scorecard was spoiled by one thoughtless soul reaching double figures.

WASTED JOURNEY

Many celebrities are ardent cricketers and film star Trevor Howard was certainly among that number. But even he must have later queried the merits of agreeing to appear in a match at Buxton, Derbyshire, on 27 July 1960. To take part, he got up at 5am and then travelled 180 miles from his home to Buxton...only to be caught at the wicket first ball.

TEN-DAY DRAW

With England one up in the 1939 series in South Africa, the final Test at Durban in March was crucial. Since the rubber was at stake, it was decreed that the match should be played to a finish. On and on it went for nine long days with proceedings being dominated by the batsmen. It had been agreed that the tenth day would be the last since the England team had to catch their ship home from Cape Town and there was no other boat for two weeks. But there seemed little prospect of a result until on that last afternoon, England launched a spectacular victory charge, reaching the stage where they needed just 42 runs for victory with five wickets standing. Then it rained...and didn't stop. After 43 hours of play, the match was abandoned as a draw. The South African Board of Control issued a statement at 5.45pm saying that, in consultation with the captains, they 'agreed that the match should be abandoned, the Board recognizing that the MCC would otherwise not have the requisite number of hours in Cape Town before sailing home.'

DEVON DUMB

Minor County Devon surpassed the expectations of all but their most cynical followers when slipping up by 346 runs in a 1990 Nat-West Trophy tie at Torquay. Somerset rattled up a record-breaking 413–4 dec. in their 60 overs. In reply, Devon could muster just 67. Most of the team were left speechless but Devon captain Hiley Edwards, calling Torquay a 'postage stamp ground', claimed: 'Even mishits were going for six. But we were pleased Somerset played the game properly and used no occasional bowlers. We wanted no charity and they gave us none.' He added defiantly: 'I must admit our players are a bit cheesed off at the moment but our defeat by 346 runs will do us no harm.'

HAMBLEDONGATE

In the days before scoreboards, the method for keeping totals was to cut a notch on a stick for every run and to make every tenth notch longer. Under this primitive calculation, Kent's match with Hambledon at Windmill Down in July 1783 was declared a tie. But it was later discovered that in one place the scorer had inadvertantly marked the 11th notch instead of the tenth. It seemed that Kent had justifiable claims for victory and indeed the faulty stick was produced in evidence. However, in what smacks of a cover-up, it was reported that 'the other scorer could not or would not produce his.'

WORST TEST BATSMAN

Few wielders of the willow could compete with Indian spinner Bhagwat Chandrasekhar who usually dealt with pace bowling from a position adjacent to the square leg umpire. In view of his timerity, it is hardly surprising that he managed four 'pairs' in Test matches.

TEACHER KNOWS BEST

In 1989, ten-year-old Zac Morris was proving more than a handful for Derby under-11s . The Barnsley schoolboy took no fewer than five wickets in his first over but, allegedly in the interests of fairness, was then barred from bowling by the teachers. No doubt the Derby teachers were especially keen on this decisive action, particularly since their team went on to win. Whether the Barnsley masters had some explaining to do later I know not, but such a magnanimous gesture would surely be a boon if introduced to the first-class game. Think how we could have prospered over the years if we had persuaded the Australians to stop Lillee from bowling because he was too quick for our batsmen.

BROTHERLY INFLUENCE

There is more than a hint of suspicion that Australian Test star George Giffen used his influence to get his brother Walter a game. Certainly Walter's on-field achievements did nothing to suggest that he was worthy of inclusion in the national line-up. Picked as an opening batsman, Walter burst up on the scene with 2 and 0 in his debut against England at Sydney in 1887. For a while he was deservedly consigned to the wilderness, only to be recalled for two Tests against W.G. Grace's tourists in 1891–92. Showing no loss of form whatsoever, Walter responded with knocks of 1, 3, 3 and 2. That would have sounded the death knell for most batsmen yet even with an average of 1.83, Walter was chosen for the 1893 touring side. Mysteriously, the selectors overlooked him when choosing the actual Test teams and so this fine cricketer was prevented from inflicting any further damage on England's attack.

NO-BALL SENTIMENTS

With England completing their victory over South Africa in the 1960 Lord's Test just after lunch on the fourth day, it was decided to arrange an exhibition match between the two teams. Far from being a harmless friendly, it once again brought to the surface doubts about the bowling action of South Africa's Geoff Griffin who, during the Test itself, had been no-balled for throwing 11 times by square leg umpire Frank Lee. If Griffin thought all that would be forgotten in the exhibition match, he was sorely mistaken. He only bowled one over – and it lasted 11 deliveries. This time it was Lee's fellow umpire, Sid Buller, who called no-ball for four out of Griffin's first five deliveries. Possibly attempting to defuse the situation, South African captain Jackie McGlew suggested to Griffin that he should bowl the remainder of the over underarm. Surely even Griffin couldn't be no-balled for that. But he was. Frank Lee promptly declared his next delivery void because Griffin had failed to warn the batsman that he was switching from overarm to underarm!

FINE LEG WORE A THREE-PIECE SUIT

A match between Yorkshire and Derbyshire at Dewsbury in 1899 was not so much affected by rain as by water in general. At the end of the second day, a mini torrent seeped through the ceiling and into the Derbyshire dressing-room after someone had left the taps on in the catering department above. Most of the players' kit was ruined, causing a hasty reappraisal of team responsibilities when Derbyshire fielded. The two players whose playing gear was relatively unscathed were forced to bowl while the other nine took to the field in their best suits. Yorkshire, who needed only 32 to win at the start of the third day, wasted no time in knocking off the required runs, the fielders being somewhat reluctant to end up with grass stains on their Sunday finery.

EXTRA HELP

Thoughtfully offering assistance to their opponents' total, the West Indies conceded a handsome 71 extras in Pakistan's first innings at Georgetown, Guyana, in April 1988. Of these, 38 were no-balls and 21 were byes. The following January in a one-day international at Brisbane, again with Pakistan, the West Indies were once more generous to a fault, giving away 59 extras, 37 of them wides.

NEVER SCORED A RUN

Over the years many claims have been advanced with regard to the world's worst batsman but one individual deserving of the most serious consideration is Somerset's A.H.S. Clark whose number of initials comfortably outscored his first-class run total. His career was confined to the summer of 1930 when in nine innings he failed to trouble the scorer on any occasion. His detractors point to the fact that he was not out a couple of times but fail to realize that, given his overall record, even if he had stayed at the crease, the outcome would surely have been the same.

WRONG LABEL

Although situated in neighbouring Wiltshire, it was deemed a good idea to stage one of Gloucestershire's 1988 Sunday League fixtures at Swindon. However, the masterplan had to be shelved when the square at Swindon became totally bald. It transpired that during the winter, weedkiller had been accidentally applied to the pitch instead of fertilizer.

BREAKDOWN IN COMMUNICATIONS

Even as fine a player as former Australian captain Bobby Simpson has had moments he might rather forget. Leading Australia in a country match in South Africa, he forgot to tell the opposing skipper that, with a lead of almost 450, he wished to enforce the follow-on. As a result, at the end of the tea interval, both teams came out to field!

HANGING ON THE TELEPHONE

The invention of the mobile phone has already begun to have an adverse effect on the peaceful world of village cricket. In 1989 it was reported that a game between Burridge in Hampshire and a Yorkshire touring team was regularly interrupted by the Burridge players' portable telephones. Indeed a number of misfields were put down to players trying to stop the ball with one hand while the phone was pressed to their ear with the other.

THREE OUT OFF ONE BALL

A match between Yorkshire Colts and Northants 2nd XI at Barnsley on 25 May 1958 produced a comi-tragic chain of events, the like of which is a rarity even in the eccentric world of English cricket. It all began when Yorkshire's Ted Lester lofted a shot to deep extra cover where fielders Jim Edmonds and Mick Norman, their eyes on the skies, unwittingly competed for the catch. It was an accident just waiting to happen. The crowd were not disappointed as Edmonds held on to the ball and in the process was knocked unconscious in a collision with Norman. For his part, Norman was concussed and, his leg spiked by Edmonds' boot, he was carted off to hospital. Edmonds subsequently recovered but the havoc caused by that single shot read: One laid out, one taken out and one given out.

THE STING

Going out to bat for Middlesex at Lord's, Patsy Hendren was half-way to the wicket when he flung his bat in the air, let out a piercing shriek and scampered back to the pavilion. He had a wasp in his box!

INJURY CRISIS

The Indian batsmen found themselves on the receiving end of some hostile West Indian bowling in the 1976 Test at Kingston, Jamaica. Gaekwad, Viswanath and Patel all retired hurt in the first innings and then Bedi and Chandrasekhar were both injured fielding. The last pair might not have been too worried about not having to face the West Indian attack again but it did mean that in their second innings, India had only six batsmen. Consequently they slumped from 97–2 to 97 all out, leaving the West Indies just 13 to win. Bedi later described the match as 'a war'.

ALL OUT FOR 0

There have been sundry instances of entire teams being dismissed without scoring but surely one of the most catastrophic was that of the Electrical Trades Commercial Travellers Association CC who were routed by Surrey villagers Bookham on 22 June 1952. What made matters worse was that Bookham needed just one ball to overhaul their opponents since the first delivery of their reply sailed through for four byes.

PREMATURE CELEBRATION

Leicestershire had been having a torrid time in the field in recent matches, spilling a number of catches, much to the disgust of their skipper Ray Illingworth. One Sunday against Derbyshire, Ashley Harvey-Walker skied a ball from Illingworth to deep mid-wicket where it was safely caught by David Gower. In a combination of relief and jubilation, Gower hurled the ball into the air. But his joy was curtailed by a swift rebuke from Illingworth, ordering him to throw it back since it was a no-ball. By the time the ball had descended from the heavens, the ricochet enabled them to run yet again although observers say that by this time the batsmen were so helpless with laughter that they were scarcely capable of standing up let alone running. The upshot of it all was that three runs came from a no-ball. Illingworth was not amused.

SOAP BAG

It is rumoured that a number of club cricketers play the game simply so that they can get away from their wives for a few hours. But there was no escape for one poor soul taking part in a match at Howick, South Africa, in March 1958. His wife telephoned the ground and insisted on speaking to him even though he was batting at the time. Thus the match was held up while he dashed to the pavilion to deal with what was obviously an emergency. And the matter of life and death? She wanted to know what he had done with the soap!

CAN WE HAVE OUR BALL BACK?

On 27 June 1990, Derbyshire and Shropshire were about to take the field for their Nat-West Trophy match at Queen's Park, Chesterfield, when embarrassed officials suddenly realised something was missing – they had no cricket ball. Even the most dedicated cricketer finds it something of a handicap to play without a ball so players and umpires had to wait in the pavilion while the balls were rushed up the M1 from Derbyshire's county headquarters at Derby over 20 miles away. After a 45-minute delay, the tie finally got under way at 11.15 am. Derbyshire chief executive Bob Lark admitted: 'Somewhere along the line there has been a breakdown in communication, but no one is to blame – it's just one of those things.'

WICKET BEFORE LEGOVER

Cricket-mad Richard Baker cancelled his honeymoon to play a match in Ripon – and was bowled first ball.

UNHAPPY EXPERIENCE

It is fair to say that Surrey's 19-year-old right-handed batsman Frederick Buckle didn't really make his mark in the match with Middlesex at Lord's in July 1869. In the first innings, he was recorded as 'absent, not sent for in time – 0' and in the second innings as 'absent unwell – 0'. Without his assistance, Surrey lost by 43 runs.

KING FORCED TO ABDICATE

Facing a crucial Dewsbury and District League match with Upper Hopton in 1978, Wakefield club Calder Grove decided to ask West Indian Test player Collis King if he would turn out for them. So imagine Upper Hopton's horror when they discovered on their arrival the true identity of the player listed as C. King. The West Indian went on to make 94 as well as taking five wickets, two catches and running a man out. Not surprisingly, Upper Hopton, beaten by some 80 runs, lodged an objection and Calder Grove were fined £1 for fielding an ineligible player and were also made to forfeit the match. Their appeal vindicated, Upper Hopton should have been in conciliatory mood but there was more than a hint of bitterness from the club official who remarked: 'Calder Grove's ground is a dump, not a patch on ours. It has no gent's lavatory.'

YORKED!

Although some allowance must be made for the fact that they had one man absent ill, Northants weren't really at their best against Yorkshire at Northampton on 8 May 1908. So dismal was their performance that they were dismissed for 27 and 15 in just 2hrs 15mins.

NO BACKBONE

Spineless batsman Pieter Marrish forfeited his wicket in a game at Johannesburg in 1972 because he spotted a snake and was too frightened to return to the crease. Meanwhile the wicket-keeper, obviously a man of steel, had ample time to remove the bails and stump him.

THE HAND OF GIL

On the eve of the 1956 Old Trafford Test, Australian wicket-keeper Gil Langley unaccountably ended up sleeping on his hand and caused so much damage to it that he was unable to play. Len Maddocks took his place but Australia should have known that it wasn't going to be their day. They were right, for this was the Test in which Jim Laker took his record-breaking 19 wickets. For the remainder of the tour a closer watch was kept on Langley's sleeping habits.

RUNNING JOKE

Luncarty's Jim McNichol greatly enlivened a Haig National Village tie with fellow Scots Manderston by running out three of his partners, including his captain, without facing a ball!

JACK WAS NO ACE

One of the briefest and least distinguished Ashes careers belonged to New South Wales opening batsman Jack Moroney who was chosen to play in one Test against England in 1950–51. In the first innings he lasted four balls until he was caught Hutton bowled Bailey from a leg glance but in the second innings he fared even worse, surviving just three deliveries before being leg before to Bailey. Moroney's Ashes career thus lasted seven balls and provided him with a pair.

WONDERFUL COLLAPSE

Few sights in sport are better than a total debacle. And that is the only way to describe the end of the Bond Worth innings in their Kidderminster League match with Cookley in July 1966. Already anticipating the glow of victory, Bond Worth were sitting pretty needing just three runs to win with five wickets standing. The deficit was further reduced when the first ball of the next over produced a single. But then in a lemming-like act of mass self-destruction, the next five balls saw the last five Bond Worth batsmen all run out, leaving Cookley the surprised winners by one run. As one Bond Worth player put it: 'I don't think our running between the wickets was as good as it could have been.'

TRUNCATED GAME

A group of boys were playing cricket at Earlwood, Sydney, in October 1962, watched from the boundary by an elephant from a nearby circus. When the ball was struck in its direction, the elephant fielded the ball with its trunk, swallowed it and ended the game.

UNSUNG HERO

One of the least auspicious cricketing careers was that of Joseph Emile Patrick McMaster who toured South Africa with Major Wharton's England team of 1888–89. McMaster batted at number nine, made a duck and wasn't called upon to bowl. And that was his solitary first-class game!

THE PERFECT GIFT

In 1989, Stuart Welch, an 18-year-old member of the MCC ground staff, won the search-for-a-spinner competition at Lord's. And the first prize was...a place on the MCC ground staff.

DIS-GUSTED

Former Warwickshire and England captain MJK Smith was facing a ball against Hampshire at Edgbaston in 1962 when a sudden gust of wind whipped his cap from his head. The headgear fell on to the stumps and he was given out 'hit wicket'.

THE PANE IS OVER

After 15 years without a win, the lads from Westmoreland Glass in Kendal, Cumbria, finally managed to scrape a three-run victory against a local cleaning firm. Hero bowler Mike Callan said: 'We could hardly believe it. We were thinking of arranging a game against an old folks' home just to get a win.'

LIFTING A THUMB

Fielding against Lancashire in July 1993, Leicestershire skipper Nigel Briers sprained a thumb when he caught it in his trouser pocket.

RUGBY UNION

LOST HIS BEARINGS

Brunei rugby player Dick Dover was nothing if not keen. So when, playing for Kukris against Panaga, he saw the opportunity to break with the ball from a scrum, he set off on a memorable 75-yard run to touch down unchallenged. He leaped to his feet in anticipation of hearty congratulations from his team-mates but was surprised to see that they appeared to be more puzzled than pleased. That was because not-so-clever Dick had been disorientated by the wheeling of the scrum and had run the 75 yards to 'score' near his own posts...

FRENCH BREAD

*G*aston Vareilles was honoured to be selected to play for France against Scotland in 1911 and enjoyed the camaraderie of travelling to the match by train with his new international colleagues. But the butterflies in his stomach left him feeling a little empty so when the train stopped at a station, he decided to jump off and buy a sandwich. However, he had failed to anticipate the possibility of a queue and returned to the platform to see the train and his team-mates disappearing into the distance. He missed the match and, apparently to his surprise, was never picked for France again.

INJURED BY HIS CAPTAIN

When the British Lions toured South Africa, skipper Willie John McBride used a novel, and sometimes painful, method of geeing up his team before a big game. He would line all the players up in the dressing room and, working his way along, would thump each man in the chest, at the same time calling out their name. The idea was that it would create a sense of purpose and unity. The ritual was duly performed prior to the Third Test but on this occasion for some reason McBride decided to hit Scotland's Gordon Brown twice. Brown had been expecting the first blow but not the second and was so badly winded that the kick-off had to be delayed while he received attention. The incident may well have broken new ground as being the first instance of a sponge man having to leave the field to go into the dressing room to treat a player before the match had even started.

TROUBLE BREWING

Devotees of humiliating defeats were cheated of a possible record in this department when the spoilsport of a referee abandoned Corby's Northern tour match at Whitby in 1989. At the time, just seven minutes of the second half had been played and Corby were already losing 80–0. The referee's decision was based upon the fact that he considered several of the Corby players were too drunk to continue. One Corby man admitted: 'We did sink a few last night.' At which point he fell over.

DANISH DISASTER

Even a totally paralytic side would have been hard pushed to equal the achievement of Danish club Lindo in 1973. These Danes were far from great as they were crushed 194–0 by a team called Comet.

MEDAL MEDDLING

The least successful attempt to decide the rightful winners of an Olympic gold medal must surely rest with the organizers of the 1920 Antwerp games. Even to this day, both France and the United States claim that they won the rugby union gold. Although staged in Belgium, the Antwerp Olympics were naturally run by the French and organized by Baron de Coubertin. France insist that the gold should be theirs by virtue of their 14–5 victory over the US at Stade Colombes on 10 October 1920. But the Americans say that match didn't count and they point to their 8–0 win against the French in Antwerp three months earlier. France dismiss that encounter, maintaining that it was a game of American Football. And anyway, they say, the kindly Baron only agreed to send a group of players to Antwerp in the first place out of the goodness of his heart and to uphold the Olympic spirit. There's plenty more years left in this one yet.

BLIND SIDE FORWARD

The 1993 Coal Board Cup tie between Nottinghamshire's Silverhill Colliery and Daw Mill from Warwickshire was held up for several minutes while players searched for a team-mate's glass eye. It belonged to 14-stone Silverhill forward Steve Bush who lost the sight of his left eye in an underground pit accident three years previously. But the search was in vain and Steve had to play the rest of the match with an empty eye socket. Although this must have been a somewhat disconcerting sight to the opposition, Silverhill still lost 17–8. Mick said: 'We had just gone down for a scrum and I was giving it a good shove. The lads reckon I was putting in so much effort that it made my eyes go pop.' Referee Peter Llewellyn added: 'I saw this player walking round staring at the ground. I asked, "What have you lost?" When he said "My eye" I thought we had a major injury on our hands.'

LACK OF COURAGE

Playing in Division Three of the Durham/Northumberland Courage Clubs Championship, Hartlepool Athletic were pipped 146–0 when they visited Billingham on 3 October 1987. A Hartlepool official confessed: 'We never really looked like winning.'

DYEING TO PLAY

There looked to be little prospect of play in the 1935 international between Uganda and Kenya at Entebbe when both teams took to the field in white shirts. While the referee pondered on the impracticality of the situation, a lady spectator suddenly raced on to the pitch carrying a vast bottle of black dye, an item which was clearly part of her everyday baggage. While all around her looked on in amazement, this resourceful individual promptly set about dyeing the home side's shirts. There was no time to allow them to dry and so with their newly-coloured kit still wet, the Ugandans played the match in black.

HISTORY REPEATING ITSELF

Supreme confidence could be said to be a national characteristic of Americans. Thus in the Hong Kong Sevens one year, the US coach had absolutely no doubts whatsoever that his team would wipe the floor with Japan. Defeat, along with quite a few other things like tactics, had never entered his head. For a start, his boys were huge whereas the Japanese were so tiny it was almost laughable. So with great expectations, he settled to watch the US kick off. The ball sailed into the air, was caught by a Japanese player and a few lightning passes later was touched down for a try beneath the American posts. With their invincibility still not open to question, the Americans tried the same thing again...with the same result. And for a third time so that after barely three minutes' play, the US were trailing 18–0. It was too much for their coach to bear. He sank to his knees and yelled to anyone who was listening: 'Pearl Harbour I can forgive, but not this!'

EARLY START

It is a wonder Fiji bothered playing any internationals after the experience of their very first overseas trip to Western Samoa in 1924. The tourists were forced to pay all their own fares and the match had to be played at the unearthly hour of 7am in order to allow the Samoans to go off to work afterwards. Just to round things off, the stadium at Apia was notable for having a large tree in the centre of the pitch which presumably made kicking-off rather a problem.

SICK LEAVE

On the morning of a France versus Scotland international in Paris, a London Scottish XV had a match arranged against a local junior side. The previous night, a number of the visiting players had been partaking of the grape and were consequently feeling a shade delicate come kick-off. Nevertheless, their prowess carried them through unscathed until ten minutes from time when their loosehead was suddenly sick all over the ball at a scrum. Until that point, London Scottish had won every single scrum but when this one also appeared about to go their way, their hooker, observing the vomit-encrusted object, decided to leave it

*and struck the ball back through the ruck of players. That
solitary scrum went to the home team, at which the visitors'
number eight called out: 'Good ball to lose, Scottish!'*

SNAKE CHARM

When the first Australian rugby union tourists came to
Britain in 1908, their mascot was a live snake. It
brought them plenty of good fortune and they remained
unbeaten. But then the snake's luck ran out – it died.
And with it went the Australians' record for they
immediately lost their next game at Llanelli.

DISGRACEFUL SCENES

Drunken rugby players were escorted from a jet after they
brawled, sang bawdy songs, told rude jokes and bared their
bottoms on a flight from Canada to London. Police met the

plane at Gatwick airport but were taken aback to discover that the rowdy players from Brampton Rugby Club in Toronto were all women.

BEATEN 200–0

Scores of over 100 in rugby union are pretty rare although there have been a few in internationals. Among the sufferers were Nigeria who lost 111–12 to Zimbabwe at Nairobi in 1987; and in 1988 Paraguay crashed 106–12 to France in Asuncion. But these are close-fought encounters compared to the English Schools' match of 20 November 1886 in which Hills Court went down 200–0 to Radford.

SOME FRIENDLY!

Right from the kick-off, a so-called 'friendly' rugby union match between Bramley and West Park Bramhope in March 1991 was marred by constant niggling among the players. Steadily, this escalated into a series of ugly brawls which culminated in referee Terry Cork abandoning the match because of persistent foul play. West Park led 4–0 at the time. All 30 players were later suspended for several weeks.

INJURED BEFORE START

About to take the field for the 1969 international with Scotland in Paris, Frenchman Jean-Pierre Salut tripped as he was running up the stairs from the dressing room to the pitch and broke his ankle. He was thus carried off before he had even made it onto the pitch.

TEETHING TROUBLES

*O*n 21 July 1964, South Africa decided to stage their
international with France away from their usual venues at
Johannesburg or Cape Town. Instead they chose the Pam
Brink Stadium at Springs, but the exercise was an
unmitigated disaster. A crowd of 25,000 was admitted, far
more than the ground could comfortably accommodate, with
the result that hardly anybody was able to see the match
properly. In protest, the crowd kept the ball whenever it was
kicked into touch. With so many replacement balls being
used, it proved an expensive match for the authorities whose
mood was not lightened by the fact that South Africa lost 8–6.
To cap it all, after the match there was a fire in the car park.

HUSBAND, WIFE AND DOG SENT OFF

*A*s a consequence of what can only be construed as some
domestic dispute, Mrs. Christine Kenyon marched on to
the pitch during the 1989 fixture between Aretians Thirds
and Bristol Saracens to remonstrate bitterly with one of the
players, her husband Mike. Receiving no satisfaction, she
deposited his kit bag and pet dog at his feet. While the other
players looked on in wonderment, the referee decided to take
firmer action and ordered the two humans and one canine to
the touch line. One spectator said of Mrs. Kenyon's
interruption: 'These days it's not often you get a woman
invading the pitch with her clothes on.'

AN ESSENTIAL INGREDIENT

*I*n 1966 Colwyn Bay RFC set off on their 50-mile journey to play
Welsh rivals Portmadoc. Once there, they got changed, the
referee ran out onto the pitch and both teams were lined up
ready for the kick-off when it was suddenly realized that
something was missing – there was no ball. So the match was
abandoned.

SOCCER

BACK FROM THE DEAD

Surely the least successful tribute in the history of soccer was that organized by HFS Loans League team Congleton. Players and spectators were forced to call off a minute's silence to mourn the death of the club's oldest fan...when he turned up at the ground. Die-hard supporter Fred Cope, aged 85, set off as usual on 27 February 1993 to watch the Cheshire club's fixture with Rossendale. Arriving at the ground, he saw the club's flag flying at half-mast but assumed it was in tribute to former England captain Bobby Moore who had died that week. But when Fred began to read the match-day programme, he was horrified to see it contained his own obituary, complete with a photograph. So as the players and the referee lined up on the pitch to pay their last respects, Fred thought he had better point out to officials that rumours of his death were greatly exaggerated. The confusion arose after another fan had innocently spread a rumour that Fred had died. Congleton manager Bill Wright said: 'We took him at his word and thought it would be nice to give Fred a tribute as he is so popular.' In a supreme understatement, he added: 'It was a shock when Fred turned up.' To underline his well-being, Fred went on to win a bottle of whisky in the half-time raffle.

TOOTH FAIRY

A tense finish to a Danish league match in April 1960 saw Norager hanging on to a 4–3 lead against Ebeltoft with just seconds remaining. Referee Henning Erikstrup was on the point of blowing the final whistle when suddenly his dentures fell out. As he ignominiously scrambled around on

the pitch in an effort to recover them, Ebeltoft equalized. Despite vehement and somewhat understandable protests from Ebeltoft, Mr. Erikstrup disallowed the goal, replaced his false teeth and promptly blew for full-time.

BASKET CASE

When the famous Harlem Globetrotters came to London in the early 1960s, among those who went to watch their unique form of basketball wizardry was Fulham goalkeeper Tony Macedo. Sadly Macedo decided to imitate their antics in Fulham's next match, against Spurs at Craven Cottage. Collecting the ball, he bounced it with either hand as he ran round the penalty-area, these being the days before the four-step law for goalkeepers. For an encore, he mimicked the clowning style of Meadowlark Lemon, pretending that he was going to throw the ball to an opponent. But just as Macedo switched his aim to team-mate Johnny Haynes, the ball slipped out of his grasp straight to the feet of the unmarked Jimmy Greaves. Macedo was left to reflect on his folly as he picked the ball out of the net.

THE LINESMAN SAW RED

We all know that linesmen not only have excellent eyesight and two parents but are completely unbiased. However some doubts do have to be expressed about the behaviour of a flag-bearer in a minor Italian league game between Tresana and Santa Anastasia. The linesman in question was an official with Tresana, a situation not guaranteed to ensure impartiality, and took exception when the referee awarded a free-kick against his club. He immediately raced on to the pitch wielding his flag and set about the entire Santa Anastasia team. In a performance of which Sylvester Stallone would have been proud, he left one player with a broken nose, another with a black eye and a third with a badly bruised face.

THANKS, REF

A Barrow shot sailing harmlessly wide struck referee Ivan Robinson and deflected into the net for the only goal of the 1968 clash with visiting Plymouth. As one Plymouth player remarked: 'It was a long way to go to be beaten by a goal from the ref.'

UNITED FANS SAW BLUE

Student Julian Fiddler sat down to watch his 21st birthday present, the video *Manchester United – Hall Of Fame*, but instead he and a mate found themselves engrossed in an American blue movie called Satin Angels. They wondered why the players started swapping shirts in the first minute. Julian said: 'We were expecting to see George Best and Bobby Charlton but we got this film of women making love to each other and couples having sex all over the place. A friend and I bought it from the Virgin store in Leeds – but there certainly weren't any virgins in the film.' Two girl students who shared the house walked out in disgust but Julian and his pal kept going well into extra-time. Virgin, who on learning of the mix-up sent Julian a genuine copy of the United film, said that the wrong label had been put on the video while it was being duplicated. All copies were removed from the shelves for checks. It was a horrible job, but somebody had to do it.

THE STRIFE OF BRIAN

Exeter City manager Brian Godfrey was so appalled with the all-round ineptitude displayed by his team during a 5–1 defeat at Millwall one Sunday in 1982 that as punishment he kept his players in London overnight to play Millwall's reserves the next day. Godfrey could only look on in anguish as Exeter even managed to lose to the Lions' second string 1–0.

BAPTISM OF FIRE

Keeping goal for Halifax Town has always been a full-time occupation, but never more so than for Steve Milton who marked his debut by letting in 13 at Stockport in Division Three North on 6 January 1934. Town lost 13–0.

STERLING CRISIS

*T*he remarkable managerial skills of the Sterling family undoubtedly played a major part in the achievements of South London boys' team Coleridge Rovers in 1992–93. With Sally Sterling at the helm and husband Fred as club chairman, the team of 11 to 13-year-olds succeeded in losing their first dozen games, conceding no fewer than 200 goals in the process. But eventually a 35–0 thrashing was too much for Fred to take and, displaying commendable ruthlessness, he sacked his wife. Fred realized there was really only one man for the job – himself. So he took over as manager and waited for the improvement. It soon came – Coleridge only lost their next match 30–0! Fred explained: 'I had to fire Sally. It wasn't her fault – she simply couldn't handle how bad we were.'

WRIGHT IDIOT

We hear many tales of goalscorers being in a rich vein where they hit the back of the net with almost monotonous regularity. The same applied to Everton defender Tommy Wright in the spring of 1972. Over a period of four days this previously unsung hero scored twice – but both were own goals. Nor did Wright choose just any old matches in which to make his mark on the scoresheet. He began on 4 March with a first-minute own goal in the fiercely-contested Merseyside derby with Liverpool at Anfield. Within a week, again selecting the opening 60 seconds as the perfect time to surprise his own goalkeeper, Wright struck once more, this time to the benefit of Manchester United at Old Trafford. Sadly, after that his career went into decline and he returned to being a perfectly competent defender.

STANDING ROOM ONLY

Members of the Falkirk sporting fraternity who thought they had better set off early for the vital Scottish Second Division basement battle between East Stirlingshire and Leith on 15 April 1939 need not have bothered. For only 32 spectators turned up – the lowest attendance for a senior league game in Britain. There were no reports of any crowd disturbances.

TAKING IT TO HEARTS

Most club directors are renowned for their generosity in defeat as they dispense Scotch and bonhomie in the boardroom after the match. Alas, Hearts director Douglas Park (no relation to Hamilton Academicals' ground) allowed his feelings to get the better of him following a hard-fought home clash with Rangers in 1988. Indeed he was so infuriated by David Symes' refereeing that he locked the match official in his changing-room for 18 minutes after the game and marched off with the key. Not altogether surprisingly, the Scottish League took a dim view of this unsporting behaviour and fined Park £1,000. He also resigned as a Hearts director.

SWIFT ACTION

Angered by the verbal derision which greeted his arrival for the match with Goldenhill Boys' Club in 1975, Glasgow referee Mr Tarbet booked all 11 Glencraig United players plus both substitutes in their dressing-room before a ball had been kicked.

SHORT-LIVED COMEBACK

Stephen Gould made the mistake of not suffering in silence as he watched his works team from Little Aston in Staffordshire lose week after week. Instead he persisted in criticizing the goalkeeper to the extent that he was finally challenged to show whether he could do any better. Gould had been a goalkeeper at school and so at the age of 40, inspired by golden oldies such as Peter Shilton and Pat Jennings, he agreed to make a less-than-eagerly-awaited comeback. 'Wearing one of the new multi-coloured jerseys and giant Sepp Maier gloves, I really felt the part as I ran out for the pre-match warm-up. I did some gymnastic exercises on the goal-line to loosen up and then jumped up and touched the crossbar.' This was his second fatal mistake for as he did so, the bar came crashing down on to his head and he was carried back to the dressing-room. He lamented: 'My comeback was over without a shot being fired.'

UNHAPPY CHRISTMAS

It takes a certain lack of discipline to be sent off after just 20 seconds, but to perform the feat on Christmas Day raises the perpetrator to the highest echelons of ineptitude. Thus Wrexham's Ambrose Brown enters the hall of fame following his swift dismissal by referee Bert Mee in the Division Three North encounter with Hull City on 25 December 1936. His one consolation could have been that he was first home for Christmas lunch.

UNWANTED AWARD

His own goal having secured promotion for Nottingham Forest in 1977, grateful Forest supporters voted Millwall's Jon Moore their Player of the Year that evening.

MISPLACED CONFIDENCE

Preston North End were one of the country's most powerful teams in soccer's formative years and accordingly they definitely fancied their chances of defeating West Bromwich Albion in the 1888 FA Cup Final. So confident were Preston that they asked to be photographed with the Cup before the game, pointing out that they were liable to be dirty afterwards and a lack of cleanliness might mar the picture. The match referee, a Major Marindin, politely inquired: 'Had you not better win it first?' Wise words, for too proud Preston lost 2–1 in what was described at the time as the greatest upset in the Cup's short history.

KEEPER FOULED BY FORD SIERRA

***B**ernie Marsh, the goalkeeper with Mid Sussex League strugglers Balcombe Reserves, had already earned a reputation for eccentricity by letting in 100 goals for the bottom-of-the-table outfit in the 1992–93 season. But he*

surpassed himself in a match at Hartfield by managing to collide with a Ford Sierra in his own goalmouth. In fairness to the hapless custodian, it wasn't exactly his fault. After all, how many goalkeepers expect to encounter a car being driven along the six-yard line while a match is in progress? It happened five minutes from time with the game delicately poised at 1–1. As play moved to the half-way line, spectator Tony Nana decided it was safe to back his car on to the pitch to turn round since his exit was blocked by other vehicles. Alas his manoeuvre coincided with a high lob being hoisted towards the Balcombe goal. As Bernie raced back, he was blissfully unaware of what was happening behind him and crashed his head into the side of the car, knocking himself out. Recovering from his ordeal, he reflected: 'The ball went up high and all I could hear was my mates shouting at me. I thought they were egging me on to save the shot and I was really determined not to let another goal in. But they must have been warning me about the car. I touched the ball over the bar and the next thing I was out cold.' The match was abandoned and from now on Bernie will be ultra-cautious in case future opponents send the Dormobile up for corners.

SCOTTISH SAGA

The least successful attempt to stage a football match must surely be that of Inverness Thistle whose second round Scottish Cup tie with Falkirk was postponed a record 29 times due to bad weather. It was eventually played on 22 February 1979, 47 days after the original date. When the beleaguered Inverness groundstaff finally got the pitch ready for play, they must have wondered whether it was worth all the effort as Falkirk triumphed 4–0. Not that Falkirk's joy lasted too long either – three days later they were knocked out of the Cup 3–0 by Dundee!

FLAG DAY

In a local league match at Bedford, referee Fred Seaton once sent off an entire team of Italian immigrants for wading into 300 spectators when somebody snatched their linesman's flag.

FLATTERED TO DECEIVE

Courage Colts were quietly confident when they took an early lead against Midas FC in an under-14 League fixture in Kent on 11 April 1976, only for Midas to strike back and run out the somewhat comprehensive 59–1 winners. And it was only a 70-minute game. The after-match inquest suggested that maybe Courage were wrong to try and sit back on their lead.

GARY'S GOOF

In the annals of goalkeeping history, the name of Leeds United's Gary Sprake is synonymous with classic displays liberally interspersed with moments of supreme incompetence. His finest hour was at Anfield in December 1967 when he succeeded in throwing the ball into his own net. Reliving the anguish, Sprake said: 'I was going to throw the ball wide to Terry Cooper when he screamed "No, no" because Ian Callaghan was closing him down. So I went to pull the ball back to my chest, as I often did, and it just flew over my left shoulder into the net. There was silence for a minute. I didn't know what to do. Jack Charlton had his back to me and was talking to the ref who then gave a goal. It happened a minute before half-time and as we were walking off, the disc jockey announced "This record is dedicated to Gary Sprake" and put on *Careless Hands* by Des O'Connor.   Sprake remains philosophical about his mishap. 'The manager Don Revie never said anything, the lads said I was unlucky and I provided Big Jack with one of his better after-dinner stories...'

CORRIGAN'S CLANGER

*O*n his day, Manchester City goalkeeper Joe Corrigan was
nearly in the same class as Gary Sprake. Corrigan peaked
in a match with West Ham when, drop-kicking from the
right-hand side of his penalty area, he screwed the ball
across the pitch straight to West Ham's Ronnie Boyce,
standing some 40 yards from goal. Boyce promptly volleyed
it back into the empty net as a bemused Corrigan looked on.

SHEEP DIP

Possibly the unluckiest mascot in the history of soccer
was Toby the sheep who was supposed to bring good
fortune to Scottish club Greenock Morton in the years
leading up to the First World War. Sadly, after one
match while the team celebrated their victory in a local
hostelry, Toby was left in the changing-room and
drowned in the players' bath.

SETTING THE RIGHT EXAMPLE

Sensing that an under-13s match at Ascot in Berkshire was
too one-sided to be interesting, the players' parents livened
matters up by starting a touchline brawl which resulted in
the police being called to separate the warring factions and
the game being abandoned. Theale Tigers were leading arch
rivals Great Holland Dynamos 6–0 when a linesman
allegedly clipped one of the players around the ear following a
bad tackle. A spectator said: 'One of the dads running the line
appeared to clip a lad. Another father ran up and had to be
restrained. Then everybody piled in. It was pandemonium.'
Tigers' secretary Jim Brown observed: 'All the boys behaved
impeccably – unlike their parents.'

TRAINER CARRIED OFF

*T*he inaugural World Cup in 1930 was notable for a fine
performance from the trainer of the United States team
during their semi-final with Argentina. Still incensed by a
controversial Argentinian goal, the US medic ran on to the
pitch to tend an injured player, yelling abuse at the referee
as he did so. In a fit if pique, he threw down his medical bag,
broke a bottle of chloroform and accidentally anaesthetized
himself. His ignominy was complete when he had to be
carried off by his own team. Not noted for their sense of
humour, the Argentinians refused to enter into the spirit of
things and went on to win 6–1.

CHAIRMAN SENT OFF

As a result of an injury crisis, 37-year-old David
Lane, chairman of Vauxhall Leaguers Tring Town,
was named as a substitute for their local derby with
Berkhamsted in season 1990–91. His moment of
glory finally arrived when he was summoned from
the bench to join the action, only to be sent off
before he had even kicked the ball!

PRINCE OF WAILS

No Welsh club has ever been Football League Champions – a
state of affairs that is solely down to the efforts of one
man, Cardiff City's Len Davies. In the last minute of the last
match of the 1923–24 season, Cardiff were drawing 0–0 at
Birmingham when they were awarded a penalty. All the
Welshmen needed to do was score and they would pip
Huddersfield for the First Division title. Naturally in view of
the significance of the kick, there was no rush of volunteers

to take it. Eventually Len Davies strode forward, placed the ball on the spot and missed. Cardiff lost out on the Championship on goal average.

IN THE SACK

*I*n 1992 the trainer of a German club was fired for
falling in love with the centre-forward. Forty-six-year-
old Roland Eybe, a coach from Delmenhorst, became
infatuated with Anja Bresch, 23, the star striker with
the women's team. He got the boot after his wife
walked out and half of the players quit because he
spent so little time trying to improve the side's
miserable record.

WORLD-CLASS LOSERS

B ulgaria have the worst record of any country in the final
stages of the World Cup. They have played 16 matches –
and haven't won one. But they are certainly pretty adept at
thinking up excuses as to why they got beaten. Following a
1993 World Cup qualifier defeat at the hands of Austria,
Bulgarian manager Dimitar Penev produced a splendid
exoneration. 'We were the victims of Austrian dirty tricks
before the game started,' he claimed with more than a hint
of indignation. 'First they hoisted a flag which was nothing
like the Bulgarian one. Then the band played a dreadful
version of our anthem. My players are a patriotic bunch and
were very angry. The team's composure and concentration
disappeared and that's why we lost.' Clearly Mr. Penev's
guidelines could be of great benefit to our own managers. It's
just a shame Doncaster hasn't got a national anthem.

THE CROWD WAS UNSIGHTED

There was huge expectancy as the Crystal Palace staged its first FA Cup Final in 1895. A crowd of 42,000, at the time a record for a game in London, turned up to see Aston Villa play West Bromwich Albion. But because of mass confusion at the turnstiles, what most of them didn't see was the game's only goal, scored within 30 seconds of the kick-off when a shot from Villa's Bob Chatt was deflected past the West Brom keeper. Thus Villa fans watched the remaining 89 minutes deprived of their moment of glory while West Brom supporters probably didn't even know their side was losing.

HELPING HAND

That old footballing adage about always playing to the whistle once rebounded on Chelsea defender John Sillett in a match against Sheffield Wednesday. Thinking the referee had blown for an infringement, Sillett caught the ball in his own penalty area but the whistle he had heard had not come from the match official but from a spectator. As the referee awarded the inevitable penalty, Sillett confessed: 'I felt the size of a pin-head.'

GOAL FAMINE

In early 1993 Third Division Hartlepool, bored with mid-table anonymity, gallantly set about shattering the endurance record for the longest spell without a goal. Following Andy Saville's last-minute penalty in the 1–0 FA Cup giant-killing defeat of Crystal Palace, they contrived to go over 13 matches without hitting the back of the net. The total stood at an impressive 1221 minutes when on 6 March at Blackpool, that man Saville had the misfortune to score

the equalizer in a 1–1 draw. His punishment was immediate:
a transfer to Birmingham City.

PAID THE PENALTY

Siminiota, a defender with Brazilian club San Lorenzo, thought he had a 2–1 victory bonus over Estudiantes in the bag when he picked up the ball in injury time believing that it had gone out of play. So he was stunned when referee Humberto Dellacasa, who had already given two hotly-disputed penalties, ruled that it hadn't – and awarded Estudiantes a spot-kick. The penalty was converted and in the resulting furore, two players were sent off for manhandling the referee who had to be escorted from the pitch by baton-wielding riot police. Really, just an ordinary game in South America.

SPOT THE BALLS-UP

The prize for the least successful attempt to organize a spot-the-ball competition goes to the Cardiff-based *Western Mail* who in January 1993 mistakenly printed the previous week's solution instead of the current poser. As a result, instead of the ball being blanked out, it loomed large in the sky. And in case readers couldn't believe their eyes, a huge white arrow pin-pointed its precise location. The contest really did live up to its slogan: 'It's so easy to be a winner.' The own-goal was spotted after 1,000 copies of the paper had been run off the presses and all but a handful were frantically withdrawn. The *Mail's* technical director admitted ruefully: 'It would have been no problem for anyone to spot that ball. I've now got a skip full of papers with the world's easiest spot-the-ball competition.'

COMYN ON STRONG

Few substitutes have made a more immediate impact than Derby's Andy Comyn, brought on in the 78th minute of the game with Bristol City at the Baseball Ground on 6 September 1992. He came on as City were awarded a free-kick near the half-way line. The ball was floated into the penalty area where Comyn rose high to head his first touch firmly into his own net past stand-in keeper Paul Williams. It was estimated that he had been on the field less than 10 seconds when he made his decisive intervention. Inspired by such benevolence, City went on to win 4–3.

LAW BREAKER

Sidelined through injury, Denis Law was forced to view Manchester United's 1968 European Cup semi-final with Real Madrid from the bench. Forgetting himself for a

moment, *Law was so excited when Bill Foulkes scored that he punched the air in his familiar style, only for his fist to smash through the roof of the dug-out. Nursing a broken bone, Law remarked: 'Marvellous. I even get injured watching the game.'*

KILLIE CRANKY

When Kilmarnock bravely entered the inaugural Scottish FA Cup in 1873, they overlooked one minor point – they were more accustomed to playing rugby than soccer. Consequently their tie with Renton in October of that year developed into something of a farce. The *Glasgow Evening News* reported that the Kilmarnock team was not 'thoroughly conversant with Association rules. On account of this, the Renton club kept the ball well up to the goal posts of their opponents as they received several free-kicks in succession thro' some of the Auld Killie's men persistently using their hands.' In the circumstances it was not altogether surprising that Kilmarnock lost 3–0.

FALSE HOPE

Few clubs have shown more commendable optimism than Fulham who, despite losing 10–0 to Liverpool at Anfield in the first leg of their League Cup tie in 1986, printed details in their programme of what would happen should the tie be all-square at the end of 90 minutes' play in the second leg. Sadly, the players failed to take the hint and Liverpool won 3–2 for an aggregate victory of 13–2.

PRAYERS WEREN'T ANSWERED

A pre-match ritual for Isadore Irandir, goalkeeper with Brazilian team Rio Preto, was to say his prayers in the goalmouth. He adopted his customary pose as Corinthians kicked off in a match at the Bahia Stadium. But he had reckoned without the renowned left foot of Roberto Rivelino who, accepting the ball straight from the kick off, blasted a shot from the half-way line. It sailed into the back of the Rio Preto net after just three seconds' play, en route whistling past the ear of a startled Senhor Irandir who was still on his knees concluding his beseechments to the Almighty.

THE REFEREE SCORED

Instructions to referees go along the lines of ensuring that the rules of the game are obeyed and keeping the score. They do not under any circumstances invite the match official to attempt to demonstrate to the players that he is a better footballer than they are. But losing control of a Sunday League fixture in Southampton, the referee became so frustrated that he decided to show off his skills instead. The game was between a local gasworks side and their bitter rivals from the electricity company. Sparks flew and the referee was taking more names than an autograph hunter. At half-time he warned the players that if they did not cut out the rough stuff, he would abandon the match. One of the gasworks players takes up the story: 'Midway through the second-half I exchanged passes with a team-mate on the edge of the penalty area when suddenly the referee pounced in between us and fired an unstoppable shot into the top corner of the net. "That," he said, "is how you're supposed to play the game." Then he tossed his whistle to a linesman and walked off the pitch, never to be seen again.' Stunned by this inspired interruption, the players allowed the game to drift to a peaceful and uneventful conclusion.

HUNG OVER

*A*s the 1908–9 season drew to a close, Leicester Fosse, already doomed to relegation from the First Division, had one thing to look forward to – the wedding of a team-mate. So they went out and celebrated his nuptials in style, the day before facing Nottingham Forest in a match crucial to Forest's safety. Fosse crashed 12–0 and the two points ensured that Forest stayed in the top flight. Suspicious of what was then a record score for Division One and between near neighbours, a Football League Commission launched an inquiry into the circumstances surrounding the match. But far from uncovering any hint of foul play or bribery, the Commission concluded that Fosse's miserable performance was solely down to the fact that they were still hung over from the wedding.

CONSOLATION PRIZE

*B*arton Athletic, beaten in all 26 matches in the Darlington and District League, were surprised to find that at the end of their dismal 1992–93 season, their efforts had been recognized with a trophy. They had won the League's fair-play award. A club official said: 'We've always been a very popular club – particularly with our opponents.'

A WISE SWITCH

As a young schoolboy in Bolton, future England centre-forward Nat Lofthouse's first game was in goal. His team lost 7–1.

NERVOUS WRECKS

Seized with a sudden spirit of adventure, Scottish club Raith Rovers decided to embark on an overseas tour to the Canary Islands in 1930. But on the way their vessel capsized and they were shipwrecked. Happily, all players and officials were rescued but thereafter Raith tended to settle for friendlies closer to home amid the less tropical climes of Cowdenbeath and Dunfermline.

WRONG TWIN SENT OFF

When Paul Pullen, a player with Diadora League outfit Bognor, became involved in a skirmish with opponents Dulwich Hamlet, the referee inadvertantly sent off his identical twin brother Mick instead. Mick, Bognor's player-manager, protested his innocence but the referee would have none of it. 'The ref called me over and gave me my marching orders,' said Mick. 'I told him it wasn't me. Paul thought it was hilarious but I'll make sure he serves the three-match suspension!'

THE PLOT SICKENS

It appears that some clubs will go to any lengths to avoid relegation but few plans have been so hopelessly ill-conceived as that of a French team from Sully-sur-Loire near Orleans. Their masterstroke was to lace the visiting side's lemonade with knock-out drops. Even the most naive referee must have suspected something when players started collapsing all around him. Thus the offending club's treachery was uncovered and they were reported to the authorities. Their punishment? Relegation.

REFEREES IN BRAWL

A game between two teams of referees in Spain should have been just about the best-behaved fixture on the calendar. But it ended in uproar after the match official sent one off and was promptly felled by a blow from the disgraced player's father, also a referee.

MORROW SORROW

Rarely has a post-match celebration gone more awry than that following Arsenal's 1993 Coca Cola Cup final victory over Sheffield Wednesday. As the Gunners' skipper Tony Adams hoisted young match-winner Steve Morrow on high, he lost his balance and Morrow crashed to the ground, breaking his upper right arm. So while his team-mates went up to collect the Cup, Morrow was stretchered off to the dressing-room, his face covered by an oxygen mask. His injury meant he missed the FA Cup final.

SALAD DRESSING

Beleaguered Chelsea keeper Dave Beasant spent the first weeks of the 1993–4 season with his right foot in plaster after dropping a jar of salad cream on his big toe, thereby severing the tendon. 'I couldn't believe it,' groaned Beasant. 'I tried to catch the falling jar with my foot. Everyone thought it was funny but it couldn't have come at a worse time for me. And the jar smashed on the floor anyway!'

SNATCH OF THE DAY

Cardiff City were jubilant after taking record receipts of over £50,000 from their FA Cup tie with Queen's Park Rangers on 6 January 1990. They were less ecstatic when they later discovered that thieves had escaped with most of the money.

HIS LORDSHIP ENTERTAINS

When Millwall moved from the Isle of Dogs to The Den on 22 October 1910, the opening ceremony was to be conducted by the distinguished Lord Kinnaird, President of the FA, before the match with Brighton. Unfortunately, while the other guests and club officials were waiting at the Cold Blow Lane end of the ground, Lord Kinnaird had inadvertantly gone to the opposite end. With proceedings ready to start, his Lordship had to be unceremoniously hauled, pushed and pulled over the wall into the ground. He then had to dash the length of the pitch without tripping over his beard. All in all, it was scarcely the most dignified of entrances.

FOOD FOR THOUGHT

A Spanish newspaper reported that a group of neo-Nazi fans had been trying to extort money from Real Madrid players in exchange for their support. This interesting precedent came to light after the Ultra Sur, who take their name from the end of the Real stadium where members hang their neo-Nazi banners, allegedly demanded 'tips' from midfielder Rafael Martin Vazquez. When Vazquez rejected their demands, it is said that gang members waited outside the locker room to 'give him a scare'. The Ultra Sur also spat at Real keeper Pedro Jaro following a UEFA Cup defeat at Paris St. Germain but these hardened thugs were persuaded to stop when an official bought them off with a plate of left-over sandwiches. Imagine the Krays being convinced to mend their ways on a promise of half a dozen sausage rolls and a tray of vol-au-vents...

POINTLESS PROTEST

A fter losing 3–1 to Darwen in the first round of the FA Cup in 1890–91, Kidderminster lodged a protest. To their delight, the protest was upheld by the FA and the match replayed. This time Darwen won 13–0!

SMASHING NEWS

Jonathan Gould, son of Coventry City boss Bobby, chose an unusual way to mark the fact that he would be taking over in goal for the League match with Southampton on 3 April 1993. Within two hours of hearing the good news, he had pranged his car twice. He reflected: 'I hope that's all my bad luck out of the way in one go.' Two weeks later, Liverpool put four past him at Anfield.

SHOW ME THE WAY TO GO HOME

Having drowned their sorrows in a bar in Cologne where their team Celtic had just lost 2–0 in a September 1992 UEFA Cup tie, soccer fans George and Pat were tired and wanted to go to bed. They hailed a taxi driver and ordered, 'Take us to our hotel.' A slight hitch was that not only couldn't the pair remember the name of the hotel, they couldn't even remember which town it was in. After careful consideration, they plumped for Dortmund, some 90 miles away. A £70 cab fare later, the boys were broke and no nearer finding the elusive accommodation. Then at 3am they had a brainwave – they rang Pat's wife in Scotland. She knew the hotel's number and the area code revealed it was another 70 miles away in Dusseldorf. Well, it began with a D. The police then organized a whip-round so that our intrepid explorers could pay their way back to Dusseldorf.

8-MINUTE WONDER

It is every player's dream to be picked for his country and West Ham United's Jimmy Barrett was no exception. But after just eight minutes of his international debut against Northern Ireland on 19 October 1929, Barrett was injured and carried off. He was never picked again and holds the dubious distinction of having the shortest England career.

PHONE GOAL

Queen's Park Rangers supremo Richard Thompson scored a £335 own goal when he rang his team's Clubcall line. After listening to the latest news about the Rangers on a car phone, he did not replace the handset correctly. The following morning when he went to get into his car ready to drive in to work, he heard manager Gerry Francis's voice still talking. The call ended up costing Thompson £335 but as he said: 'Fortunately most of the money will come back to QPR.'

BIN THE PINK

Desperate times call for desperate measures. So Torquay United, languishing in the lower reaches of the Third Division during season 1992–93 and finding themselves unable to improve matters on the field, decided to try a little psychology off it. Nothing as drastic as lifting a curse or parading the club's past trophies before every game (a very short ceremony), instead they opted to paint the away team dressing room 'sleepy' pink. The idea was that visiting sides would be lulled into tranquility by the peaceful pastel shades and on taking the field would be rendered impotent in the face of a tidal wave of warrior-like United attacks. But the colour scheme merely seemed to make United's opponents more determined and following four quick home defeats, the Devon club thought it wise to redecorate. 'The pink just didn't seem to have the desired effect,' lamented a club official.

TREBLE TROUBLE

Former St. Mirren captain Billy Abercrombie boasts the distinction of having been sent off three times in the same match, against Motherwell in 1986. Referee Louis Thow brandished the red card at Abercrombie three times – first for the original offence, the second for talking back and the final one for dissent. Abercrombie was banned for 12 matches.

FOUR OFF

*T*owards the end of a Third Division match at Northampton on 6 September 1992, spectators could be heard placing bets on how many players visiting Hereford would end up with. The lucky ones were those who chose seven. The first Hereford man to be sent off by referee Brian Coddington was Andy Theodosiou after a 72nd-minute foul. Two minutes later, assistant coach Greg Downs followed for protesting about the award of a penalty to the home side. With the score at 1–1, the nine men having equalized the penalty, Hereford's numbers were reduced to eight when David Titterton was dismissed for time-wasting. Then in the final minute, Richard Jones was despatched for a foul to complete a quartet of sendings-off in just 18 minutes. Clearly Hereford had developed a taste for the proverbial early bath since on his first game back after suspension, Titterton was sent off again, in the fixture with Wrexham. A club official admitted: 'Our discipline could have been better.'

LOSING STREAK

Stockport United FC of the Stockport Football League managed to lose 39 consecutive League and Cup matches between September 1976 and 18 February 1978. When this splendid run came to an end, it was said that players and officials didn't know whether to laugh or cry.

MOTSON BEWARE!

The subtle interviewing technique of Peruvian broadcaster Mario Sanchez spectacularly failed to endear him to his subject following a match in Lima. Ramming a microphone under the nose of 6ft 3in striker Corina, Sanchez asked him why he had missed three simple heading chances and how he thought that area of his game could be improved. Corina pondered for a moment and then announced, 'like this' before head-butting his inquisitor in the face, rendering him unconscious. Corina was arrested after a scuffle with police.

CLASSIC OWN GOAL

In a First Division game at Derby on 24 October 1992, visitors Charlton showed the value of teamwork to create a classic strike on goal. The ball was languishing idly around the half-way line when suddenly two touches, neither from a Derby player, left the ball nestling in the back of the Charlton net. First, Charlton's Darren Pitcher succeeding in slicing the loose ball high into the air and 30 yards back towards his own goal. Still there was no immediate danger, but as the ball plummeted from orbit just outside the

penalty area, team-mate Scott Minto intervened to place the deftest of headers wide of advancing keeper Bob Bolder and into the corner of the net. Many of the spectators thought it was worth the admission money alone.

SOMETHING FISHY

In days of yore, it was the practice after testimonial matches at Grimsby for players to be given cases of fish as thanks for their participation. After one such game, Tom Finney was presented with a case of plaice and Nat Lofthouse received a case of cod. Lofthouse queried this and asked the donor: 'How come Finney's got plaice and I've only got cod?' The man replied: 'Well he played better than you did tonight.'

BOSTON STUMPED

At the start of the 1992–93 season, Boston United officials discovered that the new back-pass rule was proving a costly business. As defenders tried to boot their way out of trouble, two match balls worth £40 apiece were kicked over the stand at their York Street ground never to be seen again.

GONE WEST

Manchester United's Enoch West was banned for life when he was found guilty, with other players, of fixing the result of a match with Liverpool on 2 April 1915. Because of their distinguished war records, his co-conspirators had their bans lifted after the First World War but West's remained in force for 30 years until 1945. When it was eventually lifted, he was 62 and wisely decided against a comeback.

KICKING THE HABIT

It doesn't say much for the footballing prowess of Italian celebrities that they felt compelled to object to the opposing team's strip – particularly since their opponents, Reggio Emilia, are a team of monks! Prior to kick-off, the celebrity XI bitterly complained about the monks' insistence on wearing their traditional habits for the match. One celebrity moaned later: 'It wasn't fair. The habit makes it impossible to put the ball through their legs.' In front of a crowd of 14,000, the team with God on their side won 4–3.

FASTEST SENDING-OFF

That honour rests with Bologna's Giuseppe Lorenzo who, after a mere ten seconds of the Italian League match with Parma on 9 December 1990, was dismissed for striking an opponent. Neither does our own Vinny Jones exactly hang around when it comes to incurring the wrath of officialdom. Playing for Sheffield United away to Manchester City in January 1991, he managed to get himself booked five seconds after the kick-off. But the following year, now wearing a Chelsea shirt, Jones broke his personal best with a splendid booking after just three seconds of the Cup tie with his old team-mates from Bramall Lane. Such was Jones' speed off the mark that the ball hadn't even left the centre circle before he launched himself into a reckless tackle.

A TOUCH OF THE SPRAKES

Copying professional goalkeepers is an admirable trait but is less desirable when you inadvertently recreate Gary Sprake's biggest blunder. Vaughan Tucker, a local league custodian from Lytham St. Annes, had just made what he called 'the greatest save of my life' in diving full-length to hold a penalty. Sadly, this feat of athleticism did not have a happy ending. 'My team-mates were still applauding me,' said Vaughan, 'as I got up and went to throw the ball out to the wing. But instead it slipped out of my hand and into the net. And I got thrown out of the team.'

INSIDE, RIGHT!

After reaching their local cup final, to take place on a neutral ground, prison team Lags XI from Holme House jail in Stockton, Cleveland, were kicked out because they could only play at home. Their manager moaned: 'The players asked if they could be let out with Group 4 guarding them, but were refused.'

TALK OF THE TOWN

In 1986 Buckingham Town's centre-forward was arrested by police ten minutes before an FA Cup tie, mid-way through the team-talk!

WRETCHED ROCHDALE

Rochdale have two claims for an entry into the footballing hall of fame. One of their players, John Burns, was sent off on his debut against Stockport County on 29 October 1921 and ten years later, on 7 November 1931, they overcame New Brighton 3–2 before setting off on a crowd-pleasing run of 17 straight League defeats. They didn't taste even the sweet success of a draw until 9 March 1932 when New Brighton once again volunteered to play them and charitably drew 1–1.

MISCELLANEOUS MISHAPS

TOO OBLIGING

Having won the Tour de France in 1988, Spaniard Pedro Delgado was confident of retaining his title. But he could only manage third place in 1989, principally because he lost nearly three minutes at the start in Luxembourg while he was busy signing autographs!

WORST TENNIS PLAYER

As has been intimated elsewhere in this book, Luxembourg has never been renowned for its phenomenal sporting prowess. Nowhere was this truer than in the Davis Cup where for years on end, their finest tennis players met with virtually unbroken failure. The heroic stalwart of their team was one G. Wertheim who turned out for ten successive years of Davis Cup ties and only ever won one set. He announced his arrival on the world stage in 1947 when in two singles rubbers against Belgium, he won a mere seven games. For good measure, he also lost his doubles match. Monsieur Wertheim fared even worse against France two years later when in his two singles defeats, he succeeded in winning only five games. But then in 1952, the world of tennis sat back in amazement as it appeared that Wertheim had met an even worse player than himself. For in the Davis Cup tie with Egypt at Mondorf-les-Bains, he trounced M. Coen 6–0 in the second set. Clearly the shock proved too much for our hero since he quickly lost the next two sets to go down 2–6, 6–0, 2–6, 2–6. Of course, even the great tennis players cannot continue indefinitely – there comes a time when ageing legs are simply too much of a handicap. And so in 1957, Wertheim bowed out of international competition after the tie with Poland, his exit possibly hastened by a 0–6, 0–6, 0–6 defeat to A. Licis. It was good to know that he had obviously lost none of that old ability.

GOOD FOR PLANTS?

Arriving for an exhibition match at a club near Blackburn, snooker player Dennis Taylor was greeted enthusiastically by an official at the establishment. Bursting with pride, he said: 'You'll be OK tonight, Mr. Taylor. The table is in first-class condition and I know you're going to like it.' 'Why's that?' inquired Taylor. 'Because I washed it for you specially this afternoon.' 'And he wasn't joking,' says Taylor. 'The cloth was absolutely saturated.'

THE EAGLE HAS LANDED

In recent years one man has become synonymous with the spirit of the Great British Loser. I speak, of course, of Eddie 'The Eagle' Edwards, ski jumper extraordinary. Having made last place his own in a number of events, 'The Eagle' soared in a 1989 World Cup event at Lake Placid when he finished ahead of the Dutchman Gerrit Konijnenberg on 'style'.

Taking into account non-finishers, Edwards' final placing was a remarkable 78th out of 83, causing him to remark, in the manner of season professionals: 'I kicked some butt.' Talking about this sudden improvement, he added: 'I'm going down thinking about my position, making contact, exploding on take-off, keeping my head down, getting into a good flight position. All of that is going through my mind, instead of just "Ooooh."' But it was a comfort to know that he wasn't lost to us forever. A week later he broke his collarbone in practice, admitting: 'The jump was so good and I was in such a good flight position that I started to panic.'

SCUPPERED

Peterborough Pirates ice hockey team lost 26 games in a row in the Heineken League Premier Division during season 1985–86. A club spokesman said: 'We are looking for an improvement next season.'

GREYHOUND BRAWL

The 1931 Greyhound Derby ended in chaos after one dog, Ryland R, had been found guilty of fighting. Coming round the final bend, Ryland R had 'interfered' with Seldom Led, causing the latter to finish last. Ryland R was duly disqualified and the race declared void, much to the disgust of the supporters of Mick the Miller who had been the first dog past the post, thereby completing a hat-trick of Greyhound Derbys. But the officials were adamant and a re-run was ordered from which Ryland R was banned. However, the rest between the two races was too short for five-year-old Mick the Miller and he could only trail in fourth at the second attempt.

BIG MOUTH

American tennis player Gardnar Mulloy had suggested, apparently in jest, that the draws for Wimbledon were fixed. But the committee did not take kindly to such remarks, however flippant. So for the 1949 championships, he was invited to pull the names out of the hat himself. He was out of luck since he pulled his own name out last – drawn against the No. 1 seed Ted Schroeder. So Mulloy went out in the first round and Schroeder (who was incidentally his doubles partner) went on to win the singles title.

MISSED HIS CUE

Mike Watterson was due to meet Bob Harris in a qualifying round match of the 1982 Coral UK Snooker Championships at Sheffield Snooker Centre. As promoter of the event as well as proprietor of the venue, one would have expected

Watterson to have been perfectly prepared for the contest. However, he was late for the start of the match and had to forfeit one frame.

DUTCH DEBACLE

Hugolein van Hoorn must have wondered whether it was worth making the trip from her native Netherlands to compete in the 1988 British Under-21 Open Squash Championships at Lamb's Squash Club in London. Up against Britain's Lucy Souter, the Dutch girl lost 0–9, 0–9, 0–9 in just seven and a half minutes.

UNDERWATER MAYHEM

One thing with water polo is that you don't get many pitch invasions. But there are sometimes flare-ups between rival players although few as serious as that which took place in the semi-final at the 1956 Melbourne Olympics. It was not so much the fact that both teams were just one step away from the final which caused the tension, it was more a question of the political situation at the time. For the competing countries were Hungary and the Soviet Union. The Swedish referee did his best to keep control but as the niggling increased, he decided to abandon the game because, in his opinion, it had degenerated into a 'boxing match under water'. Hungary were leading 4–0 at the time and went on to win the gold with the Russians getting the bronze.

PHLEGMATIC

An ice hockey game without a mass brawl is like a soccer match without a kick-off. Tempers ran particularly high in a clash between Montreal Canadians and Buffalo Sabres, so much so that Canadians' Denis Savard spat at an opposing player. Unfortunately, his spitting was no more accurate than his passing that night and he missed his intended target and hit one of the match officials instead. The official remained commendably cool but Savard was sent off, giving him time to clear his head as well as his throat.

TOO COLD FOR HUSKY RACING

Britain's first husky sled championships, scheduled for 28 February 1993, were called off because it was too cold for the dogs. An organizer of the event, in the Kielder Forest, Northumbria, said: 'We've had temperatures of minus nine degrees Centigrade. The ice and snow have made it far too dangerous.'

MORE PRACTICE NEEDED

The African nations may be emerging forces in many sports but Swaziland clearly weren't quite ready to take centre stage at the 1980 World Bowls Championships in Melbourne. In one match they crashed 63–1 to Japan.

ALARMED

During the 1981 World Snooker Team Cup, referee John Smyth popped out one morning to buy a new battery for his portable alarm clock. He put the clock in his jacket pocket and forgot all about it. But in the afternoon it went off mid-way through a match between John Spencer and Paddy Morgan. Proceedings were halted while Smyth rummaged around to find the off button.

HIS BOTTLE WENT

Beals Wright, the United States number one, was ruled out of the 1906 Davis Cup by a bizarre sequence of events. On the eve of the American team's departure, he made a conscious decision to get drunk, knowing that he had the long sea voyage to England on which to recover before he was again required to wield a racket in earnest. Waking up in the team hotel the following morning, he experienced that familiar sensation of a dry mouth and rang for a bottle of soda water. It arrived unopened and Wright was without a bottle opener. Instead of ringing down for one, he unaccountably attempted to open it with a toothbrush (whether he was also in the practice of cleaning his teeth with a corkscrew we do not know). The exercise was doomed to failure and the neck of the bottle smashed in his right hand. Bleeding profusely, he called out for help before fainting. Sadly, the wound became infected and Wright developed blood poisoning. Indeed, one finger had to be amputated. Needless to say, he was forced to withdraw from the Davis Cup, all because he had fancied a few drinks.

TAKING DEFEAT TO HEART

It could be argued that Myiesha Bradford of Richmond, California, over-reacted just a little when she allegedly shot and paralysed her husband Alvin in 1989 because she was angry that he had rolled a gutter ball, thereby losing a ten-pin bowling match.

FOXES ON THE RUN

The motto of Friendsville Academy Foxes basketball team was 'Humble in victory, praiseworthy in defeat'. They must have dispensed a great deal of praise between 1967 and 1973 when they managed to lose 128 successive games. The small-town American team only had one cheerleader and their tactical know-how was, to put it mildly, limited. Their coach admitted: 'I used to give them pep talks until I realized it was making them nervous.' An indication of their prowess can be gauged from the fact that a gentleman by the name of Phil Patterson was voted the club's player of the year for 1970 even though he hadn't scored a single point all season.

HOCKEY HUMILIATIONS

In a ladies' hockey international at Merton, South London, on 3 February 1923, France went down 23–0 to England. The men of India went one better during the 1932 Los Angeles Olympics when they thrashed the United States 24–1...a result which didn't go down too well with the home crowd.

FINAL FLIGHT

A racing pigeon owned by the first Duke of Wellington was released from a sailing ship off the Ichabo Islands, West Africa, on 8 April 1845. Across continents it flew, defying storms and scorching sun, until on 1 June, 55 days and at least 5,400 miles later and just a mile from its loft at Nine Elms, Wandsworth, it dropped dead.

WASHED OUT

Rarely has an event been more chaotic than the 1955 US National Men's Doubles tennis tournament. It was scheduled to take place between Monday 15 August and Sunday 21 August 1955 and for the first two days, everything

ran comparatively smoothly. Then hurricane 'Diane' hit
town and three days of torrential rain left the grass courts at
Longwood Cricket Club, Boston, looking like paddy fields. At
one stage, the water level was higher than the net posts. By
the Saturday, the day before the tournament was due to end,
the first round hadn't even been completed. Then as yet more
rain started to fall, players began to drop out. The list of
withdrawals was lengthened by the forthcoming Davis Cup
final between the United States and Australia which was due
to begin the following Friday. Seeing no end in sight at
Boston, both team captains immediately ordered their players
to scratch from the National Doubles. In total, 14 pairs
withdrew, including five from the third round and two from
the quarter-finals. One duo even dropped out at match point.
And because the courts were so damp, the matches tended to
be long, drawn-out affairs. It was an organizer's nightmare.
What remained of the tournament finally reached a
conclusion a week late, the winners being an unseeded pair
from Japan.

CAUGHT HARE

At the very first greyhound meeting at Wembley on 10 December 1927, a dog called Palatinus caught the hare before the race had finished. There had to be a re-run.

WORST NETMINDER

Richard Copland, netminder for Irvine Magnum Wings ice hockey team, made quite an impact in the 1986–87 season. He only played in two matches for the Scottish club, in the course of one weekend in November, but let in a total of 56 goals – 24 against Peterborough Pirates and 32 against Lee Valley Lions. In fact he faced just 122 shots in all, nearly half of which ended up in the back of his net. His record of conceding a goal almost every two minutes has unfortunately proved a tough act to follow.

LOWE BLOW

The hushed tones of that doyen of snooker commentators, Ted Lowe, were heard to splendid effect in a match involving Fred Davis. Faced with an awkward shot, Davis attempted to straddle the corner of the table but found the position uncomfortable and therefore switched the cue to his left hand. At which Ted informed the watching millions: 'Fred Davis is 67 years of age now and he's obviously a little too old to get his leg over.' Realizing what he had said, Ted tried to qualify his statement: 'As you can see, he prefers to use his left hand instead.'

WASTE OF ENERGY

The final of the light-heavyweight wrestling at the 1912 Stockholm Olympics was a close-fought contest. In fact it was so close that it was impossible to separate Anders Ahlgren of Sweden and Ivar Bohling from Finland...even after nine hours of wrestling. At that point, the judges decided they'd seen enough and stopped the bout, giving both men silver medals. No gold was awarded. All that effort for nothing...

A RIGHT SHOWER

The Toronto Blue Jays baseball team couldn't wait to show off their new stadium for 1989, the Skydome, the first in the country with a retractable roof. But at the opening ceremony they were caught out by a sudden downpour. None of the spectators had brought umbrellas and it took 34 minutes to put the wonder roof up, by which time everyone was soaked to the skin.

GAME, SET AND MATCH

Barely had she taken her tennis racket out of her bag than a Miss C. Wolf was putting it back again, ready to go home. For she had been beaten 0–6, 0–6 by Pauline Betz in the 1943 Tri-State Tournament at Pennsylvania. And she hadn't won a single point. A similar humiliation had befallen a Miss Huiskamp in Seattle 33 years earlier. She had battled through her encounter with Hazel Hotchkiss, also without winning a point. At least British dental student J. Sandiford managed to extract one point from his match with Australia's J.E. Harper in the 1946 Sutton Tournament. But that was all, as Sandiford fell 0–6, 0–6 in just 18 minutes.

NO SMOKE WITHOUT FIRE

The 1980 Davis Cup final between Czechoslovakia and Italy in Prague was a fiery confrontation. The Italian supporters were at their most excitable as they loudly queried what they considered to be unfair umpiring decisions. The situation boiled over in the fifth set of the match between Tomas Smid and Adriano Panatta. The score stood at 3–3 when play was held up for 45 minutes following the arrest of an Italian spectator. According to the Czech police, the offender (who it later transpired was a lawyer and the brother of a prominent Communist politician in Italy) was ejected from the hall for violating a no-smoking rule. His friends denied the charge and insisted that he had merely been cheering 'in a normal manner'. The Italian team flatly refused to play on until the man was allowed to return to his seat. Ironically it was Italy's Panatta whose concentration was wrecked by the interruption. He went on to lose the match and the Czechs took the Cup.

THE PRICE OF FAME

Having won the men's figure skating title in 1920, 1924 and 1928, Sweden's Gillis Grafstrom had high hopes of completing a four-timer at the 1932 Winter Olympics at Lake Placid. As a result of his achievements, Grafstrom was quite a celebrity at the Games and a movie camera was on hand to record his exploits. Alas, the camera literally proved Grafstrom's downfall during the compulsory figures. For it was allowed too near and part-way through his routine, Grafstrom collided with it, falling heavily and suffering mild concussion. Consequently, the hapless Swede had to settle for the silver medal behind Austrian Karl Schafer.

FAST FRAME

*P*oor Patsy Fagan found that Alex Higgins lived up to his
'Hurricane' nickname in a frame at the Irish Professional
*Snooker Championships. Higgins raced to a break of 122 and
won the frame in just 2min 45sec. One wag said it would
have been even quicker if Higgins hadn't gone for a pint half-
way through!*

MINE'S A DOUBLE

*A*bitter battle of the sexes erupted in Cornwall over
publicans' claims that women darts players were taking
too long to finish their matches. Originally, the ladies used to
have just game of 601 per match but then they insisted on
playing three like the men – and that's where the trouble
started for the Lostwithiel Darts League. Jonathan Cock, the
League secretary, said: 'The problem is they are just not good

enough to get a double to finish games. So they go on and on. I've been getting a lot of flak from landlords about ladies' matches taking so long. There will just have to be a change in the rules to try to shorten games. The men start their matches at 8pm and are finished 90 minutes later – even a bad men's match will take no longer than a couple of hours.' One landlord, who did not wish to be named, moaned: 'It's past a joke. At one match the women were still throwing at nearly 1am when the pub had closed and the staff had been sent home.'

NODDED OFF

Facing match point in his 1964 Wimbledon men's singles first round clash with South Africa's Abe Segal, American Clark Graebner hit a ball which clearly landed beyond the baseline. He waited for the inevitable call of 'out' which would signal the end of his participation in that year's competition. But none came. All eyes turned on the lineswoman, Dorothy Cavis Brown, and the reason for the silence became apparent – she had dozed off. A ball boy ran over to rouse the embarrassed official but her plight had been captured by sufficient photographers to ensure that she swiftly made world-wide headlines. She was subsequently suspended from duty and soon afterwards gave up umpiring.

MEADOWLARK YEMEN

The Yemen basketball team which took part in the 1982 Asian Games were no great threat to the Harlem Globetrotters. Their finest moment came in the match with Iraq at New Delhi. They lost by 251 points to 33.

PUTTING ON WEIGHT

Feeling confident during the weightlifting event at the 1966 Empire and Commonwealth Games, English middleweight Louis Martin asked for a weight increase in pounds. Alas, the officials thought he meant kilograms and he nearly ruptured himself attempting the subsequent lift.

IN A FIX

In 1945 the basketball team from Akron University travelled several hundred miles across the United States to play Brooklyn College in Boston. They arrived to find the game had been cancelled after members of the Brooklyn team were arrested on suspicion of fixing matches and accepting money from professional gamblers.

SLIPPERY CUSTOMER

The organizers of the 1956 Winter Olympics at Cortina D'Ampezzo in Italy must have thought they had made a safe choice by asking Italian speed skater Guido Caroli to be the last runner in the ceremonial relay for carrying the Olympic torch. However, as he completed a circuit of the arena, Caroli slipped and fell in an undignified heap. The crowd gasped but fortunately the flame didn't go out and the Olympic tradition remained intact.

SNOOKER STOPPED BY RAIN

It's not often that rain stops play in snooker but it happened during the 1973 World Championships at the City Hall, Manchester. Water seeped through the roof and onto the

"I THOUGHT THIS WAS MEANT TO BE SNOOKER, NOT POOL!"

table during the quarter-final between Fred Davis and Alex Higgins and play was halted while workmen carried out running repairs.

SEAT OF LEARNING

I am aware of a number of quaint pastimes that are performed in rural areas of Britain but the following item which appeared in 'Where and When in East Anglia' is, I believe, a first: 'Men's and Ladies' Singles, Pairs and Triples as well as Mixed Pairs are invited to the Yarmouth Bowling Green to compete for £5,000 of prize money at the Great Yarmouth Open Bowels Festival.'

FLYERS' WINGS CLIPPED

One of the biggest drubbings in ice hockey's Heineken League was the 41–2 by which Richmond Flyers crashed to Cleveland Bombers on 19 February 1983. But four years later, even that show of incompetence was surpassed by Telford Tornadoes who lost their Second Division match with Bristol Phantoms 49–3. A Telford official said: 'We were flattered by the scoreline.'

PLAYING IT COOL

The least enthusiastic demonstration of paternal pride in an offspring's sporting achievement was undoubtedly that of the father of tennis player Charlotte Sterry. After winning the Wimbledon ladies' singles for 1895, Miss Sterry cycled home to Surbiton, with her racket in a clip on the front fork. There she found her father clipping the hedge. 'Where have you been, dear?' he asked. 'To Wimbledon, of course, father,' she replied. 'Ah yes, I remember – you were playing the final, weren't you? Did you win?'

THE PRIDE OF THE PENTATHLON

The Tunisian team set new standards for the equestrian event in the Olympic modern pentathlon when they failed to score a single point in the 1960 Games at Rome. This was largely due to the fact that at some stage or another, the entire team fell off their horses. Nor did Tunisia exactly excel in the remainder of the pentathlon. One of their swimmers came perilously close to drowning and they were ordered from the shooting range because of fears that they were endangering the lives of the judges. When it came to the fencing, they were severely handicapped by only having one man who could fence. Behind his mask, the Tunisians hoped that nobody would realize they were sending out the same man over and over again. But in the course of this plucky little competitor's third contest, his opponent recognized him as the man he had just fought and had him disqualified. Tunisia came last.

IMPERSONATING A LINE JUDGE

Two of the leading lights in ladies tennis, Suzanne Lenglen and Helen Wills, met in a special challenge match at the Carlton Hotel, Cannes, in 1926. Naturally enough when the players heard the umpire, Commander George Hillyard, call 'Game, set and match to Mademoiselle Lenglen', they assumed it was all over. But with the ladies half-way to the dressing-room, the Commander had to summon them back because he discovered that Miss Wills' final shot had been called 'out' by someone in the crowd and not by the linesman, Lord Charles Hope, who indeed affirmed that the ball was most certainly in.

RIPPING YARN

Any snooker shot that required even a modicum of athleticism was always a problem for big Bill Werbeniuk. Once, playing Dennis Taylor in a Champion of Champions tournament, Werbeniuk bent over to line up an awkward shot when a vast rendering sound ripped across the hall. The Canadian had split his trousers. Werbeniuk muttered something (which, fortunately for those of a nervous disposition, was inaudible) and rushed out of the hall. Taylor was worried in case he could see the pink since Werbeniuk never wore any underpants. After lengthy adjustments, Werbeniuk returned to a wall of applause normally reserved for the World Champion or Jimmy White.

NONE TOO FRIENDLY

In the so-called 'Friendly Army Tournament' at Miskolc, Hungary, in August 1981, the USSR over-ran Afghanistan 86–2 at handball.

SOMETHING TO SHOUT ABOUT

In 1989 a 12-year-old cheerleader, Angelina Perez, reportedly gave birth to a son during the third quarter of an American Football game in Guyaco, Peru. Apparently her persistent jumping up and down and general enthusiasm for the proceedings caused her to go into premature labour. It is not known whether her fellow cheerleaders responded with cries of 'Give us a B, give us an A...'

SERVED UNDERARM

When Spain entertained Brazil in Barcelona in the second round of the 1966 Davis Cup, there were hopes of an epic singles encounter between the host nation's Manuel Santana and Thomas Koch. The first set lived up to the billing with Koch edging home 7–5 but then Santana injured his shoulder and was forced to serve underarm for the rest of the match. Not surprisingly the Spaniard was unable to inject much power or guile into an underarm serve and Koch attacked him with relish. Poor Santana lost the next two sets 1–6, 1–6, and with it the match.

REDDY TEDDY GO

A teenager threw the Northern Puppy Derby at Sunderland Greyhound Stadium into turmoil one year by lobbing a teddy bear onto the track in front of the onrushing dogs . To the disgust of punters, the dogs immediately decided that the teddy looked more appetizing than the hare and set about tearing it to pieces. Inevitably the race was declared void. At court the youth, who needed a police escort from the track to avoid retribution from the irate crowd, was fined £100. He also had his teddy confiscated.

WRONG-WAY RIEGELS

The finest moment in the history of American Football occurred in the 1929 Rosebowl when 'Wrong-Way Riegels' became an overnight celebrity. California centre Roy Riegels picked up a Georgia Tech fumble on the Tech's 20-yard line and raced down the pitch – but sadly in the wrong direction towards his own goal. As the other players looked on in stunned silence, his team-mate Benny Lom rushed over to tackle Riegels on his own one-yard line. Roy's run had brought the 53,000 spectators to their feet but it proved a costly aberration. For the move resulted in Georgia scoring two vital points which enabled them to win 8–7. Riegels said later: 'I thought the noise was the fans yelling encouragement.' Yet far from being pilloried, Riegels became an unlikely all-American hero. He received a stack of fan mail including a proposal of marriage in which he and his bride would walk up the aisle instead of down!

BREAK POINT

Tennis player Lighton Ndefwayl blamed his defeat in a Zambian professional tournament on the fact that his opponent kept breaking wind. 'It made me lose my famous concentration,' complained Ndefwayl. He also moaned that his jockstrap was too tight.

AND FINALLY...

After beating 1,000 rivals in a gruelling 500-mile race, Percy the racing pigeon flopped down exhausted in his Sheffield loft...and was promptly eaten by the neighbourhood cat. To add insult to injury, the 90-minute delay in finding his remains and handing his identification tag to the judges relegated Percy from first to third place. A truly great sporting failure.